2005

SKEPTICS ANSWERED

SKEPTICS ANSWERED

HANDLING TOUGH QUESTIONS ABOUT THE CHRISTIAN FAITH

D. JAMES KENNEDY

MULTNOMAH
BOOKS

SKEPTICS ANSWERED
published by Multnomah Books
A division of Random House, Inc.

© 1997 by D. James Kennedy

Published in association with the literary agency of Alive Communications, Inc., 7680
Goddard Street, Suite 200, Colorado Springs, CO 80920. www.alivecommunications.com.

International Standard Book Number: 978-1-59052-659-0

Printed in the United States of America

Library of Congress Cataloging-in-Publication Data:

Kennedy, D. James (Dennis James), 1930-
    How to answer the skeptics/by D. James Kennedy.
        p.cm.
    Includes bibliographical references.
    ISBN 1-57673-148-0 (alk. paper)
        1-59052-659-7 pb
    1. Apologetics. 2. Skepticism—Controversial literature. I. Title.
BT1211.K46   1997
239—dc21   97-22501
                                                              CIP

This book is dedicated to
Mary Anne Bunker and Ruth Rohm,
my efficient secretaries
who have faithfully served me
through the years.

CONTENTS

....

ACKNOWLEDGMENTS

There are several people I would like to acknowledge for their help with this book. I thank Rob Wilkins, Jerry Newcombe, and Janet Kobobel Grant for their invaluable assistance with much of the editing. Thanks to Lois Keffer for the helpful study guide. Thanks to Dan Benson of Multnomah Publishers for his vision for this book, and to the entire Multnomah staff for believing in it. Finally, I am grateful to Greg Johnson and his colleagues at Alive Communications, who made this book possible in the first place.

....

PART ONE

A
Reasonable
Faith

....

CHAPTER 1

Skeptics Are Welcome

Then He said to Thomas, "Reach your finger here, and look at My hands;
and reach your hand here, and put it into My side.
Do not be unbelieving, but believing."
JOHN 20:27

he young lady, probably in her late twenties, was baring her soul on
the radio. As the host of a radio call-in talk show, she was telling all of
Los Angeles on a Saturday night how she was losing her faith. It was
almost gone. She was debating whether to go all the way and take down
the cross that adorned her bedroom wall. After setting the stage for a
discussion of her dilemma, she invited believers and unbelievers alike to
call in and share their experiences of faith or skepticism. One of my staff
members happened to hear her and even sent her a copy of one of my
books. (But we haven't heard from her yet!)

Whether she was sincere or just putting on a radio act, this woman
represents a major portion of our society: people with a skeptical eye
toward the Christian faith. The saddest thing was that she implied that for
a person to believe, he or she must stop thinking and asking questions.
You just have to make a leap of faith—a blind leap.

My friend, nothing could be further from the truth when it comes to
the Christian faith. Christianity has answers that are not only satisfying for
the soul but also satisfying for the mind. Skeptics are welcome to the
church! Skeptics are invited to look at the Christian faith. Throughout the

ages, many skeptics have looked at Christianity's historicity and have ended up coming to faith in Christ. The evidence is there. It just needs to be looked at with an open mind.

Consider the case of Gen. Lew Wallace, the author of *Ben-Hur: A Tale of the Christ*. We know General Wallace best for this pro-Christian book, which became the basis for the 1959 film that still holds the record for the most Oscars (eleven) in film history. But did you know that earlier in his life Wallace was a skeptic? Not only was he a skeptic, but he also set out to disprove the Christian faith. After several years of intense research, he became a Christian. It would have been intellectually dishonest for him to do otherwise!

One of the best known apologists (defenders) of the Christian faith today is Josh McDowell, author of the immensely helpful *Evidence That Demands a Verdict*. But did you know that, as a college student, he was very skeptical about Christianity's historicity? In fact, he spent some time on study leave at the British Museum specifically to refute the faith. He thought the task would be simple. A slam dunk. A no-brainer. After a few weeks of intense study, he realized how wrong he was. He saw that the Christian faith is based on historical facts, available for anyone open-minded enough to discover them. After examining the historical evidence and seeing the changed lives of some college friends, he, too, became a Christian. For more than thirty years now, he has spoken all over the world to share the good news of Christ. He has argued in innumerable debates with unbelievers on issues related to Christianity, especially the historicity of Christ's resurrection, which is arguably the best attested fact of antiquity.

Skeptics are welcome. Come, let us reason together, says the Lord.

Now, please don't misunderstand me. I'm not saying we can comprehend with our minds every aspect of Christian theology—for instance, the Trinity—but I am saying reasonable answers exist for the honest skeptic. Christianity is based on "many infallible proofs" (Acts 1:3). Part of this book's purpose is to look at some of those truths and to answer some of the most common objections that unbelievers have about the Christian faith.

JESUS AND SKEPTICS

How did Jesus deal with skeptics? It's from Him that we get the phrase, "Oh you of little faith," but keep in mind He was talking to His disciples, who had witnessed miracle after miracle yet still wavered in their faith.

Look at how Jesus treated one of His disciples who showed skeptical tendencies. I refer here to Thomas, whom we often call "doubting Thomas" because of the incident that occurred after Christ rose from the dead and then appeared to His disciples:

> Now Thomas, called the Twin, one of the twelve, was not with them when Jesus came. The other disciples therefore said to him, "We have seen the Lord."
>
> So he said to them, "Unless I see in His hands the print of the nails, and put my finger into the print of the nails, and put my hand into His side, I will not believe."
>
> And after eight days His disciples were again inside, and Thomas with them. Jesus came, the doors being shut, and stood in the midst, and said, "Peace to you!" Then He said to Thomas, "Reach your finger here, and look at My hands; and reach your hand here, and put it into My side. Do not be unbelieving, but believing."
>
> And Thomas answered and said to Him, "My Lord and my God!"
>
> Jesus said to him, "Thomas, because you have seen Me, you have believed. Blessed are those who have not seen and yet have believed." (John 20:24–29)

Doubters are welcome! Skeptics are welcome! Not those who merely want to play mind games or to engage in a power trip. When Jesus stood before Herod, who demanded Jesus do miracles, He did nothing of the sort. He didn't even open His mouth. Herod wasn't seeking truth. Nor were the Pharisees. When they demanded a sign (even after He had done some incredible miracles), He would not accommodate them. We have to make a distinction here between the honest skeptic and the one who's not interested in truth. When Jesus stood before Pilate and mentioned the word *truth,* Pilate asked, "What is truth?" (implying no such thing as absolute truth existed). Not recognizing that truth stood right before him, the governor turned around and walked out. There are many Pilates today. They deny such a thing as Truth, with a capital *T,* even exists.

Because we can't judge the heart, we don't know whether a skeptic is interested in honest dialogue or just mind games. In either event, we must remember what Paul said: "A servant of the Lord must not quarrel but be gentle to all, able to teach, patient, in humility correcting those who are in opposition, if God perhaps will grant them repentance, so that they may know the truth, and that they may come to their senses and escape the snare of the devil, having been taken captive by him to do his will" (2 Timothy 2:24–26). That's our mandate: to present the truth in love so those who will may come to repentance and faith in Christ.

Are you a skeptic? Do you know someone who is? Do you ever deal with any? Would you like to be fortified in your faith and armed with facts you can share with those who falter in their faith or who don't believe? Then this book is for you.

OVERVIEW

This book contains three sections. The first section, "A Reasonable Faith," deals with questions of evidence and authority. Specifically, I deal with questions surrounding the Bible, since that's the basis for our faith. How accurate and reliable are the Scriptures? Isn't the Bible "just a collection of outdated myths," as many in our culture believe? Since most Christians attempt to answer skeptics' questions from the Bible, we must establish this amazing book's credibility. One chapter will focus on natural evidence for the Bible. A second chapter will deal with supernatural evidence for it. A third chapter will focus on our need always to be ready to defend the faith. In that chapter, I will lay some of the ground rules for debate and for apologetics.

The second part of the book, "How I Know God Exists," focuses on God's nature, meaning, and character—specifically as incarnated in His Son, Jesus Christ. We will look at arguments from philosophy, science, creation, and the Bible for God's existence. The next three chapters deal with Jesus Christ, "the visible manifestation of the invisible God." Amazingly, some people question whether Jesus even lived. Secular witnesses from antiquity will lay that myth to rest. Next, we will look at the evidence for Christ's divinity. Finally, we will look at what some skeptics say about Christ. You may be surprised.

The third section, "Answers to Common Objections," focuses on some of the issues that are raised over and over in opposition to the faith. For example: Aren't all religions the same? Don't all roads lead to God? How can Christians maintain that Christ is the only way to God?

In the following two chapters I will deal with the problem of evil and the problem of pain. How can evil exist if God is all-good, all-powerful, and all-loving? This question has plagued thoughtful people throughout the ages. Finally, we will look at the issue of life after death. Is there any evidence for it?

After this section, we will review in an epilogue the highlights of what we've looked at throughout the book. This parting chapter puts together some of the most important points from the various chapters.

HONEST ANSWERS

God has given us abundant evidence if we will but do our homework. I mentioned Lew Wallace, former skeptic and author of *Ben-Hur*. He summed up well the veracity of Christianity: "After six years given to the impartial investigation of Christianity, as to its truth or falsity, I have come to the deliberate conclusion that Jesus Christ was the Messiah of the Jews, the Saviour of the world, and my personal Saviour."[1]

I pray this book will help you as you dialogue with skeptics or if you are a skeptic. In Christianity, honest answers exist for honest questions. Skeptics are welcome!

CHAPTER 2

....

A Word about the Word

For I am not ashamed of the gospel of Christ, for
it is the power of God to salvation.
ROMANS 1:16

What is faith?" asked the Sunday school teacher.

"Oh, that's easy," replied the ten-year-old. "Faith is believing something you know is *not* true."

Unfortunately, that little boy's definition summarizes what many people think about faith. For them, to believe is to make a "leap of faith." It isn't rational but irrational.

The truth of the matter is, Christianity is a reasonable faith. It is based on a set of incontrovertible, historical facts. Contrary to being a form of intellectual suicide, given the facts, believing in Jesus Christ as Savior and Lord is the most reasonable choice one can make.

Now, I hasten to add that certain matters of faith go *beyond* reason, but they don't contradict it. As Christian author and speaker Josh McDowell has said, "Christians are not to park their brains in the church's narthex."

THE VERY WORDS OF GOD

The Holy Bible forms the foundation of our faith. It is more than a book. As Christians, we believe it to be perfect—more powerful than a split atom, more true than death and taxes, and more reliable than the most sober and studied historian. We believe, in fact, the Bible contains nothing less than the very words of God. Our faith—our very lives—are staked on the trustworthiness of the holy Scriptures.

But as we all know, not everyone believes this. The Bible, the best-selling book of all history, is also the least understood and most criticized. No other book is asked to withstand such a heavy weight of proof as the Bible. The combination of prejudice and misunderstanding is an intoxicating mix for the unbeliever, who has a desperate need to hide a diseased and rebellious heart behind a wall of denial. In more ways than one, the unbeliever's life is also staked on the Bible—that it is *wrong* about the nature of reality, that it is *wrong* about one God at the center of creation who deserves worship, and most of all, that it is *wrong* about man, who, left to himself, is on a one-way journey to hell.

With the Bible, the ante is upped, and the bet is nothing less than eternity. It is not surprising, then, that such a divergence of opinion about the Bible exists. As believers, we begin and end our understanding of the Christian faith with the Bible. In living, explaining, or defending our faith, we are most likely to say, "The Word of God says..." As believers, that settles the matter, no matter what the matter may be.

That position often seems to make us vulnerable. What happens, for example, when we are talking to someone who dismisses the Bible? How many times have you been explaining Christianity to someone, explaining God and reality from the Scriptures, when someone says, "Oh, the Bible...I don't believe in the Bible."

That comment, which is usually brought up at the beginning of the conversation, is meant to put an end to such dangerous talk. The knockout blow. The slammed door. The irrevocable can of worms. The big finito. When the truth of the Truth is dismissed, indeed it often feels to the Christian that he or she is being asked to explain the heights of heaven and earth when the only available ladder is being ripped from underfoot. It can be a very intimidating moment.

GOD'S DYNAMITE

What I would like to show, however, is that such a disbelief in the Scriptures does not have to be the end of the matter. In fact, such a comment can be used to turn what was meant as a slammed door into a revolving door of new opportunity.

First, at the risk of sparking some controversy, let me say this: I do not believe it's necessary for a person to believe the Bible to be converted. That may strike some of you as strange, but I would remind you that the apostle Paul went all over the Mediterranean basin—from Jerusalem to Spain, Greece, Turkey, and Italy—preaching the gospel to people who didn't believe the Bible.

How can this be—new converts who don't believe in the Scriptures? Isn't that an oxymoron like "jumbo shrimp" or "freezer burn"? Not necessarily.

The Greek word for *gospel* is the same root word for our *dynamite*. When someone speaks or reads the gospel, even in bits and pieces, it has tremendous power—no less than the power of God—to break down barriers, penetrate hearts and minds, and transform lives. People can believe—even partially—and be converted to the faith. In the case of many of the people Paul witnessed to, they came to believe fully in the Bible only after they were converted.

Consider this analogy. You are sleeping one night, and you hear a noise. You reach over to turn on your lamp and see a man with a mask climbing in your window. He has a knife. What do you do? You pull out your drawer, take out your gun, and say, "Stop right where you are!" and he stops. He looks down at what you have in your hand, and he says, "Oh, a gun. I don't believe in guns," and he starts forward again. It should be perfectly obvious that there is nothing you can do. He doesn't believe in guns. You are helpless. Right? Wrong! There is something you might do. Squeeze. Bang! He will instantly believe in guns.

My point is this: The Scriptures have incredible power, whether a person believes that or not. So, to a certain degree, we need to learn to relax. In some ways even our terminology is wrong. *Defending* the faith, for example, is like saying we need to defend an uncaged lion. The lion, in almost any case I can think of, will do quite nicely by itself.

What we need to learn is how to uncage the Word's power, to remove whatever obstacles we can. When an unbeliever says, "Oh, I don't believe in the Bible," it's meant as a fierce attempt to slam, bar, and lock the door in the face of such a threatening force. So what can you do?

THE JUDO TECHNIQUE

Before I became a Christian, I was professionally trained in boxing and judo. Boxing, I quickly discovered, wasn't my style. It was impossible, for example, to make it through a match without getting hit a dreadful number of times. Outside of the ring, on the streets, the opposite problem had to be dealt with. Usually, there was only one punch, and it was no fun if you weren't the person who threw it.

Judo was more my speed. I found the sport interesting and studied it for a while. Its potential power is enormous. Once, while I was in Miami, I was talking to a lifeguard who was also an instructor in judo for the Miami police department. A five-foot-six-inch guy who weighed about 150 pounds, this Filipino was nobody to mess with, as I soon learned.

While I was talking to him, he had his eye on a couple of guys in the ocean who were getting too close to some dangerous rocks. He ran to the shore and blew his whistle, signaling them away. They ignored his instructions; so he warned them again. They expressed their contempt of his warnings and went on doing what they pleased.

Finally, the lifeguard had had enough. "Come out of the water! You're done! That's it! Out!" They came out of the water, all right—one of them looked to be about six foot two inches and weighed about 250 pounds. Furious with the lifeguard, he charged him, throwing a wild punch. The lifeguard caught the guy's arm and flipped him over his head. The big man landed about fifteen feet behind the lifeguard. He lay there, flat on his back like a walrus who had fallen out of a second-floor window. Splat! In a flash, the lifeguard had straddled the man, who started to curse my friend as soon as the guy recovered his breath. The lifeguard ended any further conversation by pouring sand in the man's mouth. Needless to say, I was impressed with the power of judo.

FINDING A FULCRUM

An act of aggression—whether judo or wild disbelief—is best dealt with by throwing a person off balance. Often this means finding a way to use the force and weight of the aggressor against *him*. It means finding a fulcrum.

When a person says he doesn't believe in the Bible, I often say, "I believe you have a right not to believe in the Bible. In fact, I would fight for that right." Now, suddenly, he is off balance. That is the last thing he expected you to say.

Now is the time to launch a counteroffensive. "If you don't believe the Bible, that means you understand it. What do you think the Bible's main point is?"

Trust me, this will be good for a few stammers. Usually, the answer will come back along this line: "Oh, you know, you do the best you can and try to live by the Golden Rule and follow the Ten Commandments and that sort of thing, and...and maybe you'll get to heaven."

Now, you have him backpedaling. What was meant as a slammed door on your argument can now become a revolving door leading to further discussion.

"Ah," you say to him, "that is exactly what I was afraid of. You have rejected the Bible, which is the most important book in history in that it has been translated into more languages, published in more editions, printed in more copies, and read by more people than any other book in history. You not only have rejected it, but you also have done so without understanding its main message. It's not that you missed the bull's-eye by a few degrees, but you have missed so badly, it's almost as if you were aiming the other way."

After you let him stammer a few more times, you might want to follow up with something like this: "Now, don't you think the more intelligent thing to do would be to let me share with you the Bible's main message—how a person can have eternal life—and then you can make an educated decision about accepting it or rejecting it?"

He is just about to hit the sand on his back. You see the position he is in? He has pretended to be so superior to all the kindergarten kiddies who believe the Bible. Now, suddenly he has been discovered to have rejected the most important book in history without even understanding its main message.

You have a powerful fulcrum. Now the one-time aggressor must decide if he wants to remain in his ignorance. For someone with a good deal of intellectual pride, that is the worst place to be.

It is not surprising, then, that every time I have tried this technique, I have always received a similar answer at this point, "Oh, well, OK. Go ahead. Tell me what it is."

Sometimes—and this is on very rare occasions—the person you are witnessing to will raise the idea, "Oh, I don't believe in the Bible," near the end of your gospel presentation instead of at the beginning. To deal with this requires a different technique, which I will discuss in chapter 4, "Be Ready Always."

A BOOK AMONG BOOKS

Although the Bible receives intense criticism on many levels, most of the skepticism can be classified on two levels: the natural and the super-natural. Once you have disarmed a person who says, "Oh, I don't believe in the Bible," you can begin to deal with specific questions relating to the Bible's unique credibility. In the remainder of this chapter, I would like to focus on questions regarding the Bible's authenticity on the natural level—

that is, how does the Bible compare to other ancient works of literature? For the moment, we will put aside the supernatural elements of the Bible (I will deal with these in the next chapter) and consider how the Bible stacks up against other books.

Many skeptics believe the Bible cannot be trusted because the original manuscripts—those documents actually written by Matthew, Isaiah, Paul, etc.—do not exist. They are no longer, to use the technical phrase, *extant*. What we have, these skeptics go on to conclude, are just a few copies of a few copies. Therefore, we have no way of knowing what the original Greek or Hebrew texts actually said.

There is an element of truth here. The original autographs, penned by the authors, are indeed no longer extant. They crumbled many centuries ago. We must also understand that other ancient writings, such as those by Plato, Aristotle, and Caesar, are also not extant. We have only copies of all the great, ancient writings. The Bible is no exception.

Therefore, in judging the accuracy of ancient documents—how close they come to the original autograph (in Latin, *autographa*)—what we need to know is how many copies we have and how close they are to one another. Obviously, if you had two manuscripts and one of them said that Jesus went into a city and the other one said Jesus went out of the city, you would not know whether He went in or out, so that becomes an important issue. It's a very significant issue with many other writings.

With most of the ancient writings relatively few copies are available. For one ancient Roman writer, Cattalos, we have only three copies. With the great historian Herodotus, we have only eight copies of his writings. The same can be said of most of the other great ancient writings. We have one, two, three, five, or ten copies.

Another important factor to consider when judging the accuracy of ancient manuscript copies is the time span between the copies and the original. Here are the time spans for some of our greatest ancient writings:

Caesar and his *Gaelic Wars:* The earliest manuscript is 1,000 years
   after Caesar lived.

Demosthenes, the great orator of Greece: The earliest manuscript
   is 1,200 years after he wrote.

Plato, the great philosopher: 1,300 years.

Herodotus: also 1,300 years.

The Greek dramatists: 1,400 years.

Cattalos, the Roman writer: 1,600 years.

Homer and his classic *The Odyssey,* which you've probably read:
   2,200 years later. Yet millions of copies of this book have been
   printed. People make it into plays, motion pictures, and tele-
   vsion programs.

By these standards of antiquity, the Bible is an amazingly credible
document. We do not have two, three, or five copies, but 5,750 Greek
manuscripts of the New Testament. In various other translations we have up
to 25,000 more copies. Quotations from the New Testament are found in
the writings of virtually every one of the early church fathers—those writers
living during the first four centuries after Christ. We also have the earliest
fragment of a manuscript, the John Rylands papyri manuscript, which is a
small portion of the Gospel of John, and it is dated at A.D. 117–138. (Some
scholars, notably Adolf Deissmann, say it may date even earlier.)[1]

Drs. Norm Geisler and William Nix note: "Because of its early date
and its location [Egypt] some distance from the traditional place of
composition [Asia Minor], this portion of the gospel of John tends to
confirm the traditional date of the composition of the gospel before the
end of the first century."[2]

John wrote this Gospel, it is generally believed, sometime in the 90s;
so you have a portion of the Gospel of John not 1,000, 1,200, 1,400,
1,600, or 2,200 years later, but as few as 30 or 35 years after it was written.

We have numerous papyri manuscripts from the second and third
century, some larger manuscripts from the fourth century, and so on. No

other ancient writing—of any kind anywhere—rests on as solid a foundation as does the Bible. In fact, if we were to throw out the Bible as being textually uncertain, we would have to do away with all ancient history. We would have to say we know absolutely nothing about anything that happened in this world before A.D. 1000 because the Bible rests on a more solid foundation than any secular writing.

Scholar and author A. T. Robertson points out that "much of the New Testament can be reproduced from the quotations of the early Christian writers."[3] In fact, virtually the entire New Testament could be reconstructed from these writings alone—even if all of the more than thirty thousand manuscript copies were lost or destroyed!

The time separation between the writing of the New Testament and the first complete manuscript copies is only about three hundred years at the most, in light of our having a copy of the complete New Testament (except for Mark 16:9–20 and John 7:53–8:11) that dates to A.D. 350.[4]

The gap between when the Old Testament was written and our earliest known manuscripts is much larger than that of the New Testament. With the discoveries of the Dead Sea Scrolls in 1948, however, a complete copy of the Book of Isaiah from the first century was unearthed. When comparing this manuscript with later copies of Isaiah, we found it read verbatim with only the slightest variation (and nothing that changed the meaning of the text). The eminent scholar F. F. Bruce said of this discovery: "The new evidence confirms what we had already good reason to believe—that the Jewish scribes of the early Christian centuries copied and recopied the text of the Hebrew Bible with the utmost fidelity."[5] Author Millar Burrows added: "It is a matter for wonder that through something like a thousand years the text underwent so little alteration."[6] Through the centuries, God preserved His Word's integrity.

TRANSLATING THE PROBLEM

Another objection to the Bible's credibility is the matter of translations. The criticism usually goes something like this: "Well, you really don't even know what the Bible originally said because the New Testament was written in Greek and then it was translated into Aramaic, and from that to Syriac, and from that to Latin, and from there to German, then to French, then to Anglo-Saxon, and now into English. So, you really don't have a clue to what it originally said."

Freely translated, this argument can be summed up as follows: "I am so ignorant of the facts, I really shouldn't be opening my mouth." The issue of the number of translations, in fact, is not an issue. The New Testament was originally written in Greek; as we have already seen, we have more than five thousand Greek manuscript copies extant, and we have several million people in the world today who can read Greek. We do not have to rely on translations at all; we can read the New Testament in the language in which it was originally written. The same is true for the Old Testament. So this argument is utterly fallacious.

The Bible, at nearly any level you might wish to examine it, is an impressively credentialed work of ancient literature.

VARIOUS OBJECTIONS

Sometimes people like to pose an objection to the Bible not as a genuine question but as an excuse for them not to believe. Some objections can be answered easily, such as the one in which Peter said in Acts that Jesus "hung on a tree," whereas the rest of the Bible says He died on the cross. Well, that's easy. Peter was speaking metaphorically. The cross was made out of wood, which is derived from a tree.

One of the objections I hear the most is, "Where did Cain get his wife?" Cain, of course, was Adam and Eve's son who murdered his brother, Abel. Genesis says that Cain went to live in the land of Nod, which was East of Eden, and there he took a wife. Where did this wife come from? The answer is simple. In Genesis 5:3 we find that "Adam lived one hundred and thirty years, and begot a son in his own likeness, after his image, and called his name Seth." Then, in the next verse, it states, "After he begot Seth, the days of Adam were eight hundred years; and he had sons and daughters." It's quite obvious that Cain's wife was his sister. You might object, saying that it's forbidden in the Scriptures to marry one's sister. Yes, but we need to be careful about *ex post facto* laws—making laws after the event. The law forbidding such marriages was passed several thousand years later. You might point out, "If one marries his sister, he is liable to have a very strange child." That is true today, but evidently the gene pool was rich enough at the beginning not to constitute a problem.

In a similar way, other objections to the Bible are easily answered. If you are troubled with Bible questions like these, I recommend investing in a good resource such as Gleason Archer's *Encyclopedia of Bible Difficulties*,[7] or a much older but still reliable book, John W. Haley's classic *Alleged Discrepancies of the Bible*.[8]

REASONABLE ANSWERS

God has not left us without the answers for the deep questions of life. He has revealed Himself through the pages of the Bible.

I'm sure you've heard the story about the man who fell off a cliff, and on his way down, he managed to grab a limb sticking out from the side of the earthen wall. He wasn't a praying man, but he called out to God anyway and asked for help. Then he heard a voice saying, "Just believe— and let go." He hesitated for a moment and then said, "Uh, is there anybody else up there?" The Christian faith doesn't operate that way. It's not a matter of looking for a God who requires the least of us or who simply sounds the best of all the choices. Our faith is rational and reasonable. It's based on well-grounded facts of history. The apostle Peter sums it up by saying, "We did not follow cleverly invented stories when we told you about the power and coming of our Lord Jesus Christ, but we were eyewitnesses of his majesty" (2 Peter 1:16, NIV).

....

CHAPTER 3

Miracles and Prophecies:
Fact or Fiction?

"When a prophet speaks in the name of the LORD if the thing does not happen or come to pass, that is the thing which the LORD has not spoken; the prophet has spoken it presumptuously; you shall not be afraid of him."
DEUTERONOMY 18:22

Thomas Jefferson, the third president of the United States and one of the chief architects of the Declaration of Independence, called himself a Deist. He was, in my opinion, closer to an atheist. That might sound like a strong opinion, but listen to my reasoning.

Jefferson created his own version of the Bible, *The Life and Morals of Jesus of Nazareth.*[1] Armed with a pair of scissors, Jefferson read through the Gospels, and whenever he came to a miracle, he simply cut out the passage. His edited Bible, needless to say, looked very different from our own Gospels. Jefferson, anchored in rationalism, could not accept the supernatural of the Bible.

My question is this: If a person can't believe in miracles, then can one really believe in a supernatural God? Can you believe God created the heavens and earth? Isn't the disbelief in the supernatural, when followed to its logical conclusion, simply a statement of atheism?

If you run into a skeptic who says he doesn't believe in the Bible because of its miracles, you might try asking these questions:

Do you believe in God? If the answer is no, then at least you know you are dealing with an honest—or at least a sometimes honest—atheist. If the answer is yes, then follow up with:

Do you believe your God is different from humans? In all likelihood, the answer will again be yes.

How is your God different? In the list of answers, almost certainly, will be the idea that this God is more powerful than humans.

Did God create the world? Again, the answer, in some form or another, will most likely be yes.

If your God had the power to create the world and set all of its natural laws in motion, wouldn't that same God have the ability to perform a miracle—that is, to do something outside of what can be explained by natural laws? At this point, you have trapped the skeptic in a contradiction. If he says no, then how can he explain a God who creates, who sets the natural laws in motion? If he answers yes, then the obvious follow-up question is:

Then why do you find it difficult to believe in at least the possibility of miracles? The real problem with believing in miracles is that it forces us to deal with a supernatural God—a being powerful beyond our wildest dreams who will one day judge us righteously and in holiness. For skeptics, miracles remind them of an intimidating God. As a result, people will go to great lengths to avoid the plainly supernatural elements of the Bible. In this chapter, I have outlined three different arguments skeptics use to deal (or, more accurately, not deal) with the miracles in the Bible—allegory, myth, and superstition.

THE TROUBLE IN SWALLOWING JONAH

Let us consider one of the most famous as well as the most critiqued miracle in Scripture—the Old Testament narrative of the prophet Jonah's being swallowed by a whale. You remember the story; it's recorded in the book that bears Jonah's name. Jonah, asked by God to preach repentance to one of Israel's most despised enemies, decides to run from the divine calling. After a storm troubles the sea, Jonah is thrown overboard by his God-fearing shipmates and, the Bible says, is swallowed by some kind of large sea creature. After three days in the belly of this fish, Jonah is vomited out on shore.

Not a particularly pleasant story. Nor—some people say—an especially believable one. To listen to some critics harp, you would think you were reading the latest edition of the *National Enquirer:* "Half-boy, Half-alligator Predicts the End of the World."

Some of Jonah's most unbelieving critics are people who claim to believe in the Bible They say that Jonah is a parable or made-up story to illustrate a theological point. Usually, the conversation starts along these lines, "You don't really swallow that business about Jonah, do you?" To which I usually respond, "I don't have to; the whale already did." Then comes the response: "You really believe that Jonah was swallowed by a whale, and three days later it spit him out on the shore, and he lived to tell the story?" To which, I respond, "Yes!"

I believe the story happened as the Bible records it. Theoretically, I suppose, the story wouldn't have to be a miracle. The Hebrew word that is usually translated as "whale" doesn't necessarily mean "whale." It could mean "shark" or "great sea creature." Well-documented cases exist of both whales and sharks being opened up only to find the remains of large animals. One shark spat out a live cow on a beach in Italy some years ago. There have even been reported cases of people being found alive. Paul Harvey once told about a man in 1895 who survived a day and a half in a whale's belly. It's quite possible, even from a purely naturalistic point of view, to believe that Jonah lived inside the belly of a great sea creature.

That, however, is theory. I believe that what happened to Jonah was a miracle. How can we explain, for example, that not only did Jonah live inside the whale's belly, but also that the whale, by pure chance, happened to spit him up in Nineveh—the very place God had called Jonah to go? The text also states that God prepared a great fish just for the occasion.

At this point I am usually accused of being a "literalist," which is said in the same tone of voice as when people use the word "cocklebur." This is a common trick to enable people, even believers, to sidestep the issue of the miraculous. If it is merely a story, an allegory, then we don't need to try to explain how it happened.

The Bible, however, in very plain terms, declares the event actually took place. In 2 Kings we are told that Jonah really lived and that he was a prophet of God. No less a person than Jesus Christ said that Jonah was swallowed by a whale, and if he was three days and three nights in the belly of a whale, so should the Son of Man be three days and three nights in the belly of the earth (Matthew 12:40).

I am not a literalist. I do not believe that everything written in the Bible is to be taken literally. I don't know any educated Christian who is a strict literalist. The Bible, like any other book, is to be taken the way it was written. The opposite of literal is figurative, and every intelligent Christian knows that the Bible contains many figures of speech. It also contains allegories or parables, and these are clearly indicated when they appear. Most of the books and newspapers you read are to be taken literally, but figures of speech are also used in them. The Scriptures are no exception. We have allegories and parables, similes and metaphors.

Let me also remind you that when figurative speech is used, whether in the Bible or anywhere else, it doesn't weaken what is being said; it always strengthens. Here, for example, are two ways of saying the same thing:

• Adolph Hitler's Panzer divisions went into Poland and quickly subdued the Polish armed forces.

• Adolph Hitler, with an iron fist, smashed Poland with his Panzer divisions.

The first is literal; the second involves metaphor. Which is stronger? Obviously, the latter. All figures of speech are used to strengthen the meaning intended. The Bible, like every great work of literature, contains a full plate of various kinds of figures of speech: synecdoche, metonymy, allegory, types, symbols, enigmas, paranomasia, prolepsis, oxymoron, and prosopopoeia, to name a few. Altogether, nearly eight hundred different types of figures of speech are found in the Bible. It would be absurd, then, for someone always to take the Bible literally.

The Bible itself makes it clear how a passage is to be taken—as figure of speech or, in Jonah's case, literally. We can't simply shift gears and name a thing it is not, just because we wish to avoid the Bible's supernatural elements.

HYPING HEROES

In discussing miracles, another favorite technique of skeptics is the "mythological" or "developmental" theory. This argument revolves around the idea that, over time, a tendency exists for people to attribute miraculous happenings to great heroes. For example, Saint Xavier never mentions performing miracles in his own letters. The farther we get from his lifetime, however, the more miracles are attributed to him. With fading memory and growing fame, the blossoming of miracles increases. In other words, miracles breed in the darkness of distance and the light of greatness.

This mythological theory is interesting and often accurate. Yet in the case of the Gospels, the theory doesn't hold water. In fact, just the opposite seems to be true: The farther you get from Christ's time, the fewer miracles writers attributed to Him. Scholars agree that, of all the Gospels, Mark's is the closest to Christ's time. Mark attributes a total of twenty miracles to Jesus. In the Gospel of Matthew, a much larger writing, twenty-two references are made to miracles. In the Gospel of Luke, twenty-one miracles are mentioned. In the Gospel of John, written the latest of all the Gospels, only eight miracles are described. According to the theory, far more miracles should appear in John than in the other three Gospels.

THE THIRTEENTH FLOOR

Then there is the "superstition" theory. I'm sure you've heard some version of this one. It goes something like this: The reason ancient people attributed miracles to happenings is because they didn't understand natural law to the level we do. Because of people's ignorance, which really couldn't be helped, they were almost fated to believe in silly miracles.

But today, we're too sophisticated to believe idle superstition. The Library of Congress in Washington, D.C., contains more than 23 million volumes of information—the largest collection of human knowledge in the history of the world. Why is it, then, that the hotel across the street from that monument to knowledge contains no thirteenth floor? A twelfth floor and a fourteenth floor can be found, but not a thirteenth. Why is it that it's almost impossible to find a sailing ship that will set forth on Friday the thirteenth?

Certainly, given our advanced knowledge, we are not superstitious. Even all those psychics on television and in the newspapers who rake in billions and billions of dollars know that. We are a wise and rational people. We would never swerve our car to avoid crossing a black cat's path, and we would never walk around a ladder rather than under it.

There is nothing wrong with being a skeptic. To cast a suspicious eye on miraculous claims is appropriate, but we need to be honest skeptics. We need to have the courage to face facts should the facts clearly present themselves. Thomas, the most famous skeptic in the Bible, said, "Unless I see in His hands the print of the nails, and put my finger into the print of the nails, and put my hand into His side, I will not believe" (John 20:25).

Yet Thomas had the good sense to believe in the facts, even if they happened to be miraculous.

PATHETIC PROPHETS

When it comes to miracles, you might reason, the skeptics have the upper hand. There is no way to prove biblical miracles did indeed occur. Obviously, we haven't invented a time machine that would allow us to investigate firsthand, but we might try another approach to test the validity of miracles. If we could demonstrate that the Bible is, in some way at least, a supernatural book, then we could perhaps convince skeptics that it's capable of dealing miraculously with the human race.

In Deuteronomy 18:22, the Bible sets up a litmus test for prophecy. "When a prophet speaks in the name of the LORD, if the thing does not happen or come to pass, that is the thing which the LORD has not spoken; the prophet has spoken it presumptuously; you shall not be afraid of him." The Bible says that you will know if a prophet is sent from God when his prophecies come to pass. Otherwise, fear him not. So God gives us in the Word His own test for an inspired prophet, and that is a test of specific, fulfilled prophecy. It is also, I believe, an equation that can prove the supernatural nature of the Scriptures.

Of the twenty-six books in the world that either claim to be or have been proclaimed to be Scripture, the issue of specific, predictive prophecy is glaringly absent. It's not found in the writings of Buddha, Lao-tzu, or Confucius. In the Koran we have Mohammed making the prophecy that he will return to Mecca, which is, of course, a self-fulfilling prophecy. The reason for this lack of prophecies is that they require supernatural ability.

We all know about so-called prophets who make fools of themselves when they fail to get much right. I recall many years ago my wife had purchased one of these erudite, intellectual magazines called the *National Enquirer* because she was intrigued by the cover story: "Modern Day Prophets Make Predictions." The world's top ten seers were predicting what was going to happen in the next six months.

I stumbled onto the magazine seven months after its publication—one month after all that was predicted was supposed to have happened. These ten "prophets" made sixty-one specific prophecies in response to questions posed to them. These were all matters that could be answered by a simple "yes" or "no." Would Liz Taylor, for example, marry a younger man? Would Mohammed Ali win his fight in Zaire? Would Ted Kennedy run for president? This was not the territory of great genius. Anyone who listened to the daily news could have predicted most of these events correctly. A blind monkey could have chosen half of them right.

How many of these sixty-one prophecies did the world's top seers get right? Fifty? That would be pretty good. Forty? A little better than dumb luck. Thirty? The same as a coin flip. To my utter astonishment, they did something that amazed me. They got none of the prophecies right. Zilch. Zero. It takes a great deal of talent to beat the odds like that.

The Bible says that the prophet is only as good as his prophecy. So much for today's top prophets. Such complete failure stands in stark contrast with the Bible's prophecies. From the Old Testament alone more than 2,000 specific prophecies already have been fulfilled. There is nothing like it anywhere else in the world. Most of the 333 predictions concerning the Messiah were fulfilled in the first coming of Jesus Christ; the rest will be fulfilled at His second coming. This is astonishing and nothing less than supernatural.

Lucky Guesses?

The skeptics, of course, are skeptical. When pressed, they offer four explanations for such overwhelming accuracy:

- Lucky guesses. Even a broken clock is right two times a day, so there are, no doubt, times you can make lucky guesses. But two thousand lucky guesses in a row? That would be quite a roll, wouldn't it?
- It really wasn't a prophecy; it was history pawned off as prophecy. This would be sort of like writing the history of World War II and signing

it "Abraham Lincoln." That won't work either, for the simple reason that we know when many of these things were written. Many of them were not fulfilled until after the Old Testament was completed and translated into Latin in 150 B.C. Even an atheist would agree that no part of the Old Testament was written after Christ's birth. All of the prophecies concerning Jesus were obviously fulfilled after the prophets had long been dead. Many of the Old Testament prophecies were not fully fulfilled until three or four centuries after Christ.

• The prophecies are too vague to tell if they are fulfilled.
• The prophecies were not fulfilled. Most of the prophecies of the Old Testament can be checked by any sixteen-year-old with a good encyclopedia. The passages deal not only with the person of Christ (333 of them) but also with every nation within five hundred to one thousand miles of Israel and all of the major cities and kingdoms (about 1,500 prophecies). So anybody can find out whether or not they were fulfilled.

Let's look at a few of these fulfilled prophecies, beginning with Old Testament predictions about Jesus. We must understand that Christianity is rooted deeply in the Jewish culture and faith. Jesus was not a Christian but a Jew. The Old Testament, in more senses than one, is pregnant with Jesus Christ. Once, I remember witnessing to a Jewish man, who said to me he did not believe in Christ.

"I'm sorry to hear that," I said to him. "Since He is the Messiah of the Jewish people who was promised in the Old Testament, you have rejected your own Messiah."

The Old Testament prophecies concerned the coming of the promised Messiah, a person who would provide salvation for Israel. I shared with this Jewish man some of those predictions:

• "All those who see Me ridicule Me; They shoot out the lip, they shake the head, saying, 'He trusted in the LORD, let Him rescue Him;

let Him deliver Him, since He delights in Him!" (Psalm 22:7–8).

- "They also gave me gall for my food, and for my thirst they gave me vinegar to drink" (Psalm 69:21).

- "Surely He has borne our griefs and carried our sorrows;… But He was wounded for our transgressions, He was bruised for our iniquities.… And the LORD has laid on Him the iniquity of us all" (Isaiah 53:4–6).

- "[In Galilee of the nations] the people who walked in darkness have seen a great light; those who dwelt in the land of the shadow of death, upon them a light has shined" (Isaiah 9:2).

- "Even my own familiar friend, in whom I trusted, who ate my bread, has lifted up his heel against me" (Psalm 41:9).

- "Then I said to them, 'If it is agreeable to you, give me my wages; and if not, refrain.' So they weighed for my wages thirty pieces of silver. And the LORD said to me, 'Throw it to the potter'—that princely price they set on me. So I took the thirty pieces of silver and threw them into the house of the LORD for the potter" (Zechariah 11:12–13).

- "I gave My back to those who struck Me, and My cheeks to them who plucked out the beard; I did not hide My face from shame and spitting" (Isaiah 50:6).

- "They pierced My hands and My feet" (Psalm 22:16b).

- "My God, My God, why have You forsaken Me? Why are You so far from helping Me, and from the words of My groaning?" (Psalm 22:1).

- "They divide My garments among them, and for My clothing they cast lots" (Psalm 22:18).

- "He was numbered with the transgressors, and He bore the sin of many, and made intercession for the transgressors" (Isaiah 53:12b).

- "They will look on Me whom they pierced" (Zechariah 12:10b).

- "And they made His grave with the wicked—but with the rich at His death" (Isaiah 53:9a).

- "Nor will You allow Your Holy One to see corruption" (Psalm 16:10b).
- "You have ascended on high, You have led captivity captive; You have received gifts among men" (Psalm 68:18a).
- "For the Gentiles shall seek Him" (Isaiah 11:10b).

When I finished reading the Scriptures to this Jewish man, I asked him, "Who are these people talking about?"

He responded, "Obviously, they are talking about Jesus."

I said, "Right, it's perfectly obvious, isn't it?"

"Yes, it was Jesus," he said to me. "So what?"

"All of the texts I just read you," I said to him, "are from the Old Testament. They were completed some four hundred years before Jesus Christ was born. And even you, a Jew, just told me it was obvious these verses were about Jesus Christ."

The man was stunned. He demanded to see the passages with his own eyes, and I showed them to him. In the 333 texts that make predictions about Jesus Christ, 451 details are delineated about his life. How do you explain that, if the Bible was not inspired by God? Isn't this proof the Bible is a supernaturally accurate book?

TOWN AND COUNTRY

The Bible is also accurate in its more than fifteen hundred predictions concerning cities and countries. More than one hundred specific prophecies in the Old Testament concern the great city of Babylon alone, but the Bible makes some amazing predictions about other countries as well. Take Egypt, for instance. At one time, Egypt was the greatest nation in all of the world. It was the king of nations. It was the richest country on earth; it was glorious.

To show how detailed and remarkable the prophecy is, let us consider just one prophecy about Egypt, which is recorded in Ezekiel 30:13b. "There shall no longer be princes from the land of Egypt."

Until a few decades ago, before Egypt went to a democratic form of government, Egypt was always ruled by a prince. History records, however, that during the nearly twenty-five hundred years between this prophecy and Egypt's change to democracy, its princes were never Egyptian. That would be like prophesying today that an American will never again be president of the United States, and then having two and a half millennia pass with no American presidents.

It's hard to imagine, isn't it? How could anyone, by law, be president without being an American? This story may seem too unbelievable to be true, but I'm not making it up—history confirms the fulfillment of the Ezekiel prophecy. Constantine Volney, a great skeptic who was responsible for the early skepticism of Abraham Lincoln, wrote of Egypt after a trip there: "Deprived 2,300 years ago of her natural proprietors, Egypt has seen her fertile fields successively prey to the Persians; the Macedonians; the Romans; the Greeks; the Arabs; the Georgians; and at length, the race of Tartars distinguished by the name of Ottoman Turks; the Mamelukes soon usurped the power and elected a leader."

After Volney's time, in the last century, Mohammed Ali (not the boxer) established the princedom again in Egypt. One might expect that an Egyptian would at last come to the throne after twenty-three hundred years, but that was not the case. The prince was born in Macedonia. His father was an Albanian aga, or commanding officer, in a Muslim country. After this, Egypt was ruled successively by the French and the English.

Even the skeptic Edward Gibbon confirms this testimony when he states, "A more unjust and absurd constitution cannot be devised than that which condemns the natives of a country to perpetual servitude under the arbitrary dominion of strangers and slave."

Even though this is just one prophecy in a book filled with prophecies, it shows how specifically, and to what detail, the predictions are actually fulfilled. Lucky guesses? Hardly.

PICK AN ATOM, ANY ATOM

To any open-minded person—honest skeptics included—the incredible fulfillment of prophecies found in the Bible attest to its divine revelation. Only God, who knows the future, could have revealed it to those who wrote down these predictions.

Lee Strobel, former legal affairs editor for the *Chicago Tribune* and a former skeptic, looked into this matter and was shocked to see the compelling evidence of just forty-eight of the prophecies about Christ being fulfilled. He eventually became a Christian, and today he is an associate pastor of Willow Creek Community Church in suburban Chicago. In a recent book, Strobel wrote a chapter called "A Skeptic's Surprise" in which he said: "I concluded that the odds of forty-eight Old Testament prophecies' coming true in any one individual are the same as a person randomly finding a predetermined atom among all the atoms in a trillion trillion trillion trillion billion universes the size of our universe!"[2]

As Strobel and scores of other skeptics have figured out, the Christian faith is based on a set of incontrovertible facts.

....

CHAPTER 4

Be Ready Always

But sanctify the Lord God in your hearts; and be ready always to give an answer to every man that asketh you a reason of the hope that is in you with meekness and fear.

1 PETER 3:15, KJV

A young pastor who was at the very beginning of his ministry decided he had no need to prepare sermons. He remembered the scripture (taken out of context) that the Holy Spirit would supply the words when needed. So he was neither worried nor prepared. His first Sunday, he moved to the pulpit and read the text he had selected. As he prayed urgently for words of wisdom, all that came to him was the inner conviction that he had been lazy and slothful for not preparing a message. Somehow he stumbled through the next half-hour, but never again did he stand before a congregation unprepared.

"Be prepared" is the motto of the Boy Scouts. In a similar way, we as Christians are to be prepared. As 1 Peter 3:15 instructs, we are always to be ready to give an answer to the honest skeptic as to why we believe what we do. Unfortunately, many Christians can't even tell others *what* they believe, much less *why* they believe.

On the other hand, some Christians question whether we should even be concerned about preparing to explain our faith. They think skeptics will never be convinced by logic. For now, let me suggest that this issue really boils down to two factors: (1) How open-minded is the skeptic? and

(2) What information about Christianity is he or she being given? More about that later.

Unfortunately, some well-meaning Christians are far from ready to give an answer to honest skeptics' objections, thereby reinforcing the unbelievers' view that Christians are ignorant and uninformed. Thankfully, many Christians are willing to take the time to learn how to answer objections. Reading this book indicates that you may be one of them!

In this chapter we will look at some of the basic tenets you need to know in order to tell others why you believe. We'll explore the reasons why your faith is logical and rational. As we do so, remember that God's Word is paramount in our discussions. It's the place we start, and rightly so, for the Bible has proven to be historically accurate and textually sound.

"RECAPPING OUR TOP STORY"

To highlight and expand on what we learned in the last two chapters, the evidence for the textual authenticity for the Bible is overwhelming. As we have seen, the Bible is beyond comparison from both historical and super-natural perspectives. On one level, no other ancient document has so many manuscript copies which are so close in time to the original auto-graphs. On another level, no other document—ancient or contemporary—can make the claim that the Bible can about fulfilled, specific prophecy.

F. F. Bruce, the great New Testament theologian, said that the evidence for the New Testament writings is far greater than any other work of litera-ture. Compared to the writings of Plato, Aristotle, Homer, or Chaucer, the Bible is far more textually credible. Any serious scholar, secular or Christian, who studies the issue would be forced to reach the same conclusion.

Sir Frederic Kenyon, the former director of the prestigious British Museum, said this about the New Testament's unparalleled textual credi-bility: "The interval then between the dates of original composition of the

New Testament and the earliest extant evidence becomes so small as to be, in fact, negligible, and the last foundation for any doubt that the Scriptures have come down to us substantially as they were written has now been removed. Both the authenticity and the general integrity of the books of the New Testament may be regarded as finally established."[1]

On a supernatural level, the Bible is filled with prophecy that has been fulfilled to its most minute detail. In the last chapter we looked at Old Testament prophecy concerning Egypt. Many predictions were made regarding the destruction of cities and kingdoms. Yet in describing Egypt's future, the Bible says, "they shall be there" (Ezekiel 29:14, KJV). This is truly an incredible prophecy considering all the descriptions of the utter obliteration of other locales. These are some of the prophecies concerning Egypt:

- "And there they shall be a lowly kingdom. It shall be the lowliest of kingdoms; it shall never again exalt itself above the nations, for I will diminish them so that they will not rule over the nations anymore" (Ezekiel 29:14b–15).
- "'The pride of her power shall come down. From Migdol to Syene those within her shall fall by the sword,' says the Lord GOD" (Ezekiel 30:6).
- "They shall be desolate in the midst of the desolate countries, and her cities shall be in the midst of the cities that are laid waste" (Ezekiel 30:7).
- "I will make the rivers dry, and sell the land into the hand of the wicked" (Ezekiel 30:12).
- "There shall no longer be princes from the land of Egypt; I will put fear in the land of Egypt" (Ezekiel 30:13).

Have the prophecies been fulfilled? After the defeat of Antony, Augustus Caesar found such wealth in Egypt that he paid all the debts he had incurred during the war. Still the wealth of Egypt was so great that

Alexandria continued to be the largest and most prosperous city in the Roman Empire during the next six hundred years.

A hundred years later, the Muslim hordes attacked Egypt and conquered it. They were overwhelmed by the sight of the cities' magnificence and wealth. Future invaders were still astonished at Egypt's wealth until finally the country was reduced to a state of abject poverty and international bankruptcy. This led to the Anglo-French domination of Egypt. Isn't it amazing that the Muslims, who are among the greatest enemies of the cross, actually fulfilled Judeo-Christian prophecies? God uses even the wrath of man to praise Him.

Clearly the Bible was written by that One who knows the future and to whom all things are open and plain. It's the very Word of the Living God. If any other book had just a small percentage of the fulfilled prophecies the Bible does, it would be considered above reproach. Yet the Bible is consistently attacked as myth or as food for the foolish.

FOOLISH HEARTS

With such strong credentials, both natural and supernatural, why is the Bible so often attacked and dismissed? Part of the reason, certainly, is that people's hearts and minds are in rebellion against God. Romans 1:21 describes the human condition: "Although they knew God, they did not glorify Him as God, nor were thankful, but became futile in their thoughts, and their foolish hearts were darkened." To admit to the Bible's impeccable credentials would be to admit God's holiness, but humanity's rebellious nature finds this option unacceptable.

Well, if people's hearts and minds are in rebellion against God, what's the sense in using logic to convince skeptics of the Bible's truth? The apostle Paul said that he was "set for a defence of the gospel" (Philippians 1:17, KJV), and he instructed Timothy to "study to show thyself approved" (2 Timothy 2:15, KJV). So clearly we are to prepare to logically present Christianity to the skeptic. Yet at the same time we are laying the foundations of evidence, we need to be praying that God, through His Holy

Spirit, will divinely and supernaturally reveal the truth to the skeptic's sin-dimmed mind and heart.

The next question I can hear you asking is "OK, but how much evidence is enough?" Given the natural prejudice of a sinful mind and heart to reject the truth, how far must Christians go to prove their case? That is a much tougher question, with no simple answer. What I will try to provide are some guidelines and principles about using evidence and some general laws of logic to help you build your arguments.

Armed with these, you must present your case in a clear, compelling way, liberally salting your presentation with prayer. Be sensitive to God's leading as to how open-minded each skeptic is. Listen for God's direction as to when to speak and when to stop.

Agnostics, those who claim to be uncertain about whether God exists or not, are, by very definition, lacking knowledge. Thomas Huxley, who is often credited with popularizing Charles Darwin's theory of evolution, is the person who first coined the word *agnostic*. It springs from the Greek root word, *gnosis,* which means "knowledge." "A" is the alpha primitive, like "un." So *agnostic* means, if you will, "un-knowledge." That, of course, is the Greek etymology. The exact Latin equivalent of *agnostic* is "ignoramus." It means precisely the same thing. So the next time you run into an agnostic, you might say, "Oh, you're an ignoramus, are you? That's too bad." Then again, you might not be fond of wearing a black eye.

Paul had something to say about agnostics long before Huxley used the word. "I would not have you ignorant, brethren," Paul said (Romans 1:13, KJV). The word for "ignorant" is *agnoses;* Paul is saying he does not want us to be agnostics because the wondrous thing about Christianity is that we *can* know. We don't have to be in the dark when it comes to believing in God and His wonderful provision for us.

LOGIC'S LIMITS

The first principle to remember when preparing to "answer every person who asks" is this: Logic has its limits. Logic, in fact, can be used to reach an illogical conclusion. Zeno, the ancient Greek philosopher, used logic to "prove" that any and all motion is impossible. For example, to get from here to the door, Zeno said you have to first travel half the distance from here to there. Isn't that correct? Any logical person would agree. A problem occurs in that, before you can travel half the distance, you have to travel half of that distance, or one-fourth the distance to the door. Before you can travel one-fourth the distance, you have to travel half of that distance, or one-eighth of the way to the door. Does anyone disagree with this? Before you travel one-eighth of the distance, you have to travel one-sixteenth. Since that process may be carried on ad infinitum, it is clear you cannot move at all. This is known as Zeno's paradox. Logically, all motion is impossible; yet, experientially, I know I can move. I can prove it by simply walking to the door.

My point is this: Logic can be manipulated. We must be extremely careful how we defend our faith and how we listen to skeptics' "logic." If we, whether believer or skeptic, bring to logic a predetermined course that it should take, we are likely to be dishonest with the evidence and manipulate the facts to suit our conclusion.

Yet within the boundaries of an honest discussion of evidence, certain laws of logic can be applied effectively. The following few pages will explain some of the most important laws of logic that help guide us to well-reasoned conclusions about the Christian faith.

CONSIDER THE EVIDENCE

Simon Greenleaf is considered by many to be the greatest expert on evidence the world has ever known. Greenleaf, the Royal Professor of Law at Harvard during the latter half of the nineteenth century, has been praised universally for his knowledge. The London *Times* said that more light on jurisprudence had come from Greenleaf than from all the jurists of Europe combined. The chief justice of the Supreme Court said that Greenleaf's testimony is the most basic and compelling that can be accepted in any English-speaking court in the world. In other words, when it comes to the question of what constitutes evidence, Greenleaf's credentials are impeccable.

His one inviolable principle in his classrooms at Harvard was this: Never make up your mind about any significant matter without first considering the evidence. That was, and is, a very good rule to follow. Greenleaf was not a Christian. In fact, he was a Jew. He did not believe in Christianity. He did not believe in Christ. He did not believe in the resurrection.

One day, the subject of religion came up. This was not surprising to Greenleaf. He knew that law was based on ethics, and that ethics and morals are rooted in religion. A discussion of religion in a law classroom was as natural as dissecting a frog in biology. When the subject of Christ's resurrection came up, Greenleaf said he didn't believe in it. One bold student raised his hand and said, "Yes, Professor, but have you considered the evidence?"

Greenleaf was honest enough to admit to himself that he, indeed, had not. He was aghast. He had lost enough face to depopulate China, so he decided to undertake such an investigation.

He examined every thread of evidence he could find on Jesus Christ and, in particular, His proclaimed resurrection. Finally, Greenleaf wrote a book on his findings entitled *The Testimony of the Evangelists,* in which he considered the evidence presented by the writers of the four Gospels— Matthew, Mark, Luke, and John. His conclusion: If the evidence for Christ's resurrection were presented to any unbiased jury in the world, they would have to conclude that Jesus of Nazareth rose from the dead. Through the examination of such evidence, Greenleaf became a Christian.

Christianity, he said, demands no more evidence than is readily conceded to every branch of human science. He added, this same amount of evidence will not necessarily be interpreted in the same manner. In *The Testimony of the Evangelists* he quotes Bishop Wilson: "Christianity does not profess to convince the perverse and the headstrong, to bring irresistible evidence to the daring and profane, to vanquish the proud scorner and afford evidence from which the careless and perverse cannot possibly escape. This might go to destroy man's responsibility. All that Christianity professes is to propose such evidence as may satisfy the meek, the tractable, the candid, and the serious inquirer."[2]

Yet, Greenleaf goes on to say, fact is still fact and evidence is still evidence—regardless of its "religious" source: "This is the question in all human tribunals in regard to persons testifying before them. We propose to test the veracity of these witnesses by the same rules and means which are there employed in our courtroom. The importance of the facts testified and the relations to the affairs of the soul in the life to come can make no difference in the principles and the mode of weighing the evidence. It is still the evidence of matters of fact, capable of being seen and known and related as well by one man as another."[3]

Greenleaf concludes that Christianity is, in fact, the only evidential, historical religion in the world and that the Christian faith rests on evidence—evidence he found so compelling and so overwhelming that any honest person examining it with an open mind would, like himself, be inescapably drawn to accept it.

THE AUTHENTICITY OF THE ANCIENT

Greenleaf went on to set forth his first rule of legal evidence concerning the Bible or any other ancient document. Listen to this: "Every document apparently ancient, coming from the proper repository or custody, and bearing on its face no evident marks of forgery, the law presumes to be genuine and devolves on the opposing party the burden of proving it to be otherwise."[4]

The Scriptures, Greenleaf concluded, had come from the proper repository—that is, it had been in the hands of persons of the church for almost two thousand years, and it bore, on its face, no evident marks of forgery. Therefore, the law presumes it to be genuine. For those who would presume the Scriptures to be other than genuine, the burden of proof falls on them to demonstrate its falseness. In other words,

Christians, in a legal sense, do not have to prove the Scriptures to be true. Instead, skeptics have to prove Scriptures to be false. That is what the law says. That is one limit to the amount of evidence we must present. When a skeptic asks you to prove that the Bible is true, you might want to gently point out to him that, legally, the burden of proof is on him to prove it untrue.

THE LAW OF NONCONTRADICTION

The most basic of all the rules of logic is the "law of noncontradiction." This is not a rule man created, although most of the great thinkers going all the way back to Aristotle recognized its fundamental truth. When God, the logos, created the universe, He set in motion the law of noncontradiction as well as other natural laws. Because of this law, which springs from God's essential nature, the cosmos is logical and rational.

The law of noncontradiction is this: "A" cannot be "A" and "non-A" at the same time and in the same sense. This is a law everyone ought to learn because we are often confronted with apparent contradictions, and this rule helps us to determine if they really are contradictions.

In understanding this law, it's first important to note the two modifiers: "A" cannot be both "A" and "non-A" at the same time and in the same sense. For example, I cannot be both Jim Kennedy and John Smith at the same time in the same sense.

Logically, can I be both dead and alive at the same time? Yes, I can. There will, in fact, come a time when some of you will probably be standing there looking at my dead body, and you will have concluded that I have died. I will at the same time be more alive than ever. You see, I will be both dead and alive at the same time but not in the same sense. I will be physically dead but spiritually alive.

Can I be both dead and alive in the *same* sense? Yes, I can. I could, for example, be both spiritually alive and spiritually dead. Before a person believes in Christ, the Bible says that individual is spiritually dead in sin, but after conversion, the person is "born again"—the spirit becomes alive.

So, in the same sense, a person can be both spiritually alive and dead, but—and here is the law of noncontradiction—not at the same time.

That's the law of noncontradiction, the most fundamental law of our existence in this world. *"A"* cannot be *"A"* and *"non-A"* at the same time in the same sense. When presenting—or evaluating—any kind of evidence, it's critical to keep this law of logic in mind. It's the second limit on the evidence we offer—this time the limit is on the *type* of evidence rather than on the quantity.

THE BOTTOM LINE

Another law I would like to discuss is that logic must be anchored in some final truth. It's the third limit to the evidence we offer. Many skeptics' arguments logically fall into what is known as the "law of infinite regression," which is the opposite of the final truth.

Let me give an example. In the next chapter I will examine the brilliant refutation of evolution by Dr. Francis Crick, the Noble Prize–winning scientist who is credited with codiscovering DNA. By examining one cell's complexity, Crick concluded it would be impossible for that cell to have evolved, even if one assumed the earth has been around for four and a half billion years. In a lay person's terms, Crick's scientific conclusion about even the possibility of evolution was "No way, Jose." Couldn't happen.

Yet despite his brilliant arguments, Crick went on to create a new theory called "Directed Panspermia."[5] That's a phrase you ought to know—*pan,* which means "all," and *spermia,* which means "sperm." Crick's theory states that some sperm of an advanced living race somewhere in the galaxy seeded the human race on earth. This is a currently popular theory, which is being taught in many colleges today.

There is—at the very least—one problem with Crick's theory. That flaw is connected to the law of infinite regression.

The obvious question by any person not totally numb between the ears is: Where did this advanced race that seeded life on earth come from? The answer, of course, might be some other more advanced race in some other part of the galaxy seeded that race. That race, in turn, was seeded by an even more advanced race, and so on, ad infinitum. In logic, this is called an "infinite regress." It simply moves the discussion out of the scientific realm into science fiction by never asking the bottom-line question that would resolve the issue rather than make it circle back on itself.

In fact, a *Star Trek* episode some years ago was based on this idea, and the people who did the seeding were discovered. Of course, they never asked the obvious question: Where did those original seeders come from? The point of the episode was that we are all, in one sense or another, brothers and sisters, or at least cousins, and that all of us—humans and Klingons and Vulcans—should stop fighting and love one another. As infinite regression shows, "logic" can often be manipulated to a predetermined end.

READY AND WILLING

Part of "being ready always" is understanding the laws of logic—the limits of logic, considering the evidence, the authenticity of ancient documents, the law of noncontradiction, and the law of infinite regression—and using them to advance the truth. The other part of preparation is being wary of using—or skeptics' using—these laws to circumnavigate the truth.

One of the key turning points in the early days of the creation/evolution conflict came in the form of a university debate between Bishop Samuel Wilberforce (son of the famous Christian statesman William Wilberforce) and Thomas Huxley. As the story goes, Wilberforce was poorly prepared, but Huxley had done his homework. Huxley bested Wilberforce and, for the first time, evolution gained a major foothold in academia, from which it has never retreated. The debate was a watershed event. Now I don't want to fix the blame for the whole evolution debacle on Wilberforce. Individuals, consciously or unconsciously needing to justify their sin, gladly latched onto anything that sounded like a plausible way to dismiss God, lest He interfere with their lifestyles. Nonetheless, we don't want to be "unprepared" as Wilberforce was. When we dialogue with skeptics, we need to do our homework and be prepared. The eternal state of people's souls are at stake.

PART TWO

How
I Know
God Exists

CHAPTER 5

....

What Does God Look Like?

For since the creation of the world His invisible attributes are clearly seen, being understood by the things that are made, even His eternal power and Godhead, so that they are without excuse.
ROMANS 1:20

One day in a grade-school art class, before God was kicked out of the public schools, a little boy was drawing eagerly. The curious teacher came by and asked, "Johnny, what are you drawing?"

Johnny looked up from his half-finished masterpiece and said, "I'm drawing a picture of God."

"But, Johnny," replied the teacher, "no one knows what God looks like."

Johnny beamed. "They will now!"

Who is God, and what does He "look like"? What do we know of His nature, His character? How do we even know He exists? To find answers to these questions, we have to look to His Word. What makes the Bible the book of the month, the book of the year, and the book of eternity is that it reveals God to the human race. The Bible is saturated with God.

From Genesis through Revelation, our faith rests in the firm belief that God is the creator, sustainer, redeemer, and sovereign Lord of all that is. Nothing that is came to be without the great *I AM*. All things, both living and inanimate, owe their existence to the God who has always been and always will be. Every act of history is noticed and directed by God to a predetermined end. So powerful is He that He can create true freedom and yet, in the end, bring the cosmos to its knees. Without God, there would be nothing. Not even nothing. There would be no reason to write this book—because I would not exist to write it, the paper would not exist to print it on, you would not exist to savor every word, and there would be no skeptics to attempt to convince.

DOES GOD EXIST?

Yet for many people, God is nothing more than a myth. They say He does not exist, or at the very least, there is no evidence for His existence. What always gets me about people who claim there is no God is that the very tongue they use to make such a statement was created and waggles and spits out blasphemy by God's power. How sadly ironic atheism is.

Still, there are many people who earnestly ask the question, "How do you know there even is a God?" That is the most basic of all objections to the Christian faith, and it's asked in a number of ways.

I used to chuckle sometimes at the late Carl Sagan, the pop astronomer who is most associated with his popularization of evolutionary views as well as the way he used to say "billions and billions." Sagan had a series about the cosmos on public television. When questioned about God, he usually said something condescending like, "Well, I'm not saying I know there is no God. It's just that if there is, there isn't any evidence for it."

Sagan is perhaps an icon for our age of stubborn, rebellious unbelief. The Bible states, "For since the creation of the world His invisible attributes are clearly seen, being understood by the things that are made,...so that they are without excuse" (Romans 1:20). Here is a man who had delved deeply into the cosmos's mysteries, who had gazed endlessly at the wonders of God's works. Yet this man did not believe in God. I am reminded of Psalm 14:1: "The fool has said in his heart, 'There is no God.'"

Although Sagan claimed to be an agnostic, a person who is unsure about God's existence, his own words seem to align Sagan's worldview more closely to that of an atheist. In the first sentence of the first episode of his cosmos series, he stated unambiguously his belief: "There is not and never has been anything in the universe but matter." That is as clear a statement of atheism as one could ever hear.

WHO CREATED LIFE?

When Sagan said there is no evidence for God, he should have taken a closer look at himself in the mirror. Literally. Life—even a blasphemer's life—owes its existence to God. God is as plain as the nose on Sagan's face. There would be no life in this universe if God had not created it. Despite what the scientists might tell you, no viable option has been offered to explain where complex living organisms came from. The only credible answer is God, a supernatural Being, who is powerful enough to bring forth life.

The age's current pseudo-answer is that all living beings are the product of evolution. Yet evolution is merely a hypothesis, and one with an increasing number of holes in its foundational logic. In fact, scientists slowly are coming to realize that life—even at the level of a single cell—is far too complex to have evolved.

In this chapter I would like to look at the research and findings of two different scientists, neither of whom, to my knowledge, is a professing Christian. Both of these scientists have come to the conclusion, based on the laws of probability, that evolution cannot account for even the simplest of living organisms.

The first scientist is Dr. Francis Crick, whom I mentioned in the previous chapter. Although his argument for panspermia—the idea that human life was seeded by a more advanced race—violates logic through the law of infinite regression, his original work, which disproves evolution, is nothing less than brilliant.

Crick, along with Dr. James Watson, is credited with the discovery of DNA, that double helix building block of life that forms like two twisted circular stairways in each of the several trillion cells of a person's body. The

DNA contains all of the information for the various parts of our bodies, as well as for every cell. This is the most complex molecule that has ever been discovered. Though it is tiny, it exists inside the nucleus of each microscopic cell. If you could stretch it out, it would be about six and one-half feet long. All of the DNA in just one human body, linked together and stretched out, would reach to the moon and back. That makes it a phenomenally complex substance.

Crick, who won the Noble Prize for his discovery of DNA, decided to ascertain the probabilities of such a complex molecule's coming into existence by the law of chance, which governs evolutionary theory. We need to keep in mind that Charles Darwin, who gave birth to the idea of evolution one hundred years ago, was operating under the assumption that the simple cell really was simple. The cell is so complex, in fact, that one evolutionary scientist said that any machine man has made, or ever will make, will never compare in complexity. That's quite a statement, given computers that can process several million bits of information in a second or two.

ALMOST A MIRACLE

Crick never progressed very far in his probability test. His first question to investigate was: What are the probabilities of a single molecule of DNA coming into existence by chance? His conclusion: 0.0 percent chance, even considering the supposed four-and-a-half-billion-year history of the Earth. Crick wrote, "An honest man, armed with all the knowledge available to us now, could only state that in some sense, the origin of life appears at the moment to be almost a miracle."[1] Despite more than seventy-five years of teaching that life came into being through evolution, Crick said that it could never have happened. Never. The idea that various amino acids in the ocean got together in primordial slime and somehow formed a single cell was preposterous. He was forced to conclude that life came about by some other process. That's when he developed the equally absurd theory of panspermia, even though no scientific evidence existed for such an idea. It was either that or believe in God.

Consider that the average human body is comprised of 30 trillion cells. Consider also how much information is stored in each cell. Dr. Walter Brown points out, "The genetic information contained in each cell of the human body is roughly equivalent to a library of 4,000 volumes."[2] As author Erwin Lutzer observes, "If we multiply that by 30 trillion, we can begin to appreciate the complexity of a single human being."[3] Yet Carl Sagan saw no evidence for God in the universe!

FAT CHANCE

Sir Fred Hoyle is the second scientist I would like to consider. Hoyle, a professor at Cambridge and one of the leading astronomers and scientists of our time, decided to test the laws of probability even further. He wanted to find out the probability of just one cell—not just one strand of DNA—coming into existence by chance.

To be fair, he even started his calculation with the supposed age of the universe—15 to 20 billion years, give or take a billion or so—rather than the supposed age of the Earth, 4.5 billion. This was an enormous advantage to the side of chance. On the other hand, because it was based on the age of the universe, Hoyle could not resort to the theory of panspermia, simply because there could be no advanced race outside of the universe. This universe, for better or worse, is the only one we know of. If an advanced race existed, it would have to be within the "confines" of this universe.

Hoyle worked with another world-famous mathematician and astrophysicist, Chandra Wickramasinghe, to calculate the probabilities. These two great mathematical minds came up with this number of years for just one simple cell to come into existence by chance: $10^{40,000}$ (10 to the 40,000th power) years.[4]

Now, I'm sure most of us have no concept how large a number $10^{40,000}$ really is. Let me try to give you some perspective. One noted Swiss mathematician, Lecomte duNouy, said that any number in which the probabilities were greater than 10^{50} would simply never happen, even cosmically.[5] Why did duNouy choose that particular figure? Because if we counted all the electrons in this universe—the thing we have the most of—the number of electrons would come to 10^{52}. That would be counting every electron in every planet, in every sun, in every galaxy. So duNouy assumed that, once something hit 10^{50}, it simply was not going to happen. That's 10^{50}, not $10^{40,000}$. How big is $10^{40,000}$? Well, take all of the electrons in the universe—10^{52} power—and multiply it times ten, making 10^{53}. Multiply this by ten, making 10^{54}. Keep multiplying this way until you have reached $10^{40,000}$. It's beyond our abilities to even imagine. That's how long it would take to produce one cell by chance. Can evolution scientifically account for the creation of life? It gives new meaning to the phrase "fat chance."

Wickramasinghe states, "Living systems could not have been generated by random processes, within a finite time-scale, in a finite universe."[6] Hoyle and Wickramasinghe, in fact, rejected evolution as the source of life. Instead, they said that for any kind of life to exist anywhere in the universe, it must be there by the hand of an *eternally existent being of infinite power, which, if you desire to, you may call God.* These two scientists concluded that if life cannot spontaneously begin, it must have a creator. Hoyle, once an atheist, became a believer in God. What other logical conclusion could he have come to?

How many millions of young people, sitting in our educational institutions, have been lied to and told that cells formed by mere chance? Just place a couple of amino acids together, toss them into a primordial slime, throw in some lightning or something, and BINGO! Instant life, instant cells. I'm being facetious, of course, but isn't it just about that ridiculous? Such hypotheses show to what extent people will go to explain away the existence of the Creator of life.

WHO MADE GOD?

God's existence is a fundamental issue. Yet once a person comes to believe in God, other questions arise. What would such a Creator look like? What kind of character would He have? How could He, being eternal and invisible, exist in time and space? Who made God? Because God is not "altogether like us," as the psalmist puts it, questions arise.

Often the first question, which is connected to the issue of eternity, is Who made God?

A seminary professor I know once received a call from the mother of a six-year-old boy who had asked that same question. The professor told the woman, "Tell him that nobody made God. God has always existed and always will."

She responded by saying, "But he won't understand that. He is only six years old."

"That's all right," the professor told her. "He won't understand it when he's sixty either, but it's still true."

Nobody made God. God is a self-existent being who has existed eternally—always has and always will exist. Of course, the boy's question is asked from a human point of view, as a mere creature and not the Creator. Everything that boy knew was made by someone. His father made the boy's tree house and built the doghouse. Some contractors built their house. Some people in Detroit made their car. Who made God? It seemed a perfectly logical question for him.

Just because his question seems logical doesn't mean his mother's answer would be illogical. To say that God is a self-existing, eternal being is contrary to no laws of logic. Nothing is unreasonable or irrational about that, unless we must suppose that everything is a creature such as we are. Furthermore, nothing is unscientific about that view. The idea of an eternally existing being violates no known scientific law. Rather, as Hoyle and Wickramasinghe demonstrated, just the opposite is true. Not to believe in God, given the reality of life in the universe, is irrational.

WHAT WAS GOD DOING BEFORE HE CREATED THE UNIVERSE?

Young people are especially curious about this question. Have you ever wondered what God was doing before He created the universe? Again, this question arises from our inability, stuck as we are in time and space, to understand eternity. Still, it's an interesting question.

Deuteronomy 29:29 tells us, "The secret things belong to the LORD our God, but those things which are revealed belong to us and to our children forever, that we may do all the words of this law." This, in a sense, is a kind way of saying, "None of your business." God has not chosen to reveal everything to us—either about Himself or about His creation. Part of this, no doubt, is because we, being finite, limited, and sinful, simply could not comprehend all truth.

Yet these things are both true: God has existed eternally, and the universe is finite in both space and time. Time as we know it was a part of God's creation. There was a time when there was no time, and there is coming a time when the great angel of God will reach out his hand, take hold of the wheel of time, and stop it. Then time shall be no more. What existed before the universe's creation we do not know, let alone what God would choose to do before He unfurled the cosmos. Now, if we wanted to, we could speculate. If we did, we should realize we are playing games and we have no idea if anything we are saying is true.

If I were to speculate, the first thing I would consider is what God was not doing. He was not sitting around twiddling His thumbs waiting for you and me to come along to make life interesting. What in the world (make that "nonworld") could He have been doing? He could have been creating other universes—billions and billions of universes, forever and ever. We don't know that this is the first and only universe God ever created. He hasn't seen fit to tell us about that. He may have been enjoying relationships with His Son and the Holy Spirit, two infinitely wise and eternal Beings.

You ask, "What would they have been talking about all this time?" About an infinity of things. They would never run out of things to talk about.

What was God doing before He created the universe? One theologian responded to the question by saying, "He was creating hell for people who ask stupid questions like that." That, of course, is the not the right answer either.

Personally, I think God was busy. In Deuteronomy 29:29 you will notice what God determines to be important to us: the things that *have* been revealed: "but those things which are revealed belong to us and to our children forever, that we may do all the words of this law."

ROCK REMOVAL

Another question connected to one of God's attributes—His omnipotence—revolves around a paradox. Could God make a rock so big He couldn't move it? To me, this is like asking, "Did you drive to work today or did you pack a lunch?" We are now in the territory of mind games, and generally the skeptic who asks this question is more concerned with creating confusion than in asking honest, searching questions about God.

Still, it's provocative. The Bible says God can do all things and nothing is impossible for Him. If that is true, says this questioner, then can He make a rock so big He can't move it? The person has asked the question in such a way that God loses regardless of the answer given. The problem, then, is the question itself, which is designed to entrap. Furthermore, I think we should remember that just because God *can* do all things doesn't mean He *will* do them to prove His capabilities.

God will never do anything contrary to His own nature. So, when we say God can do all things, we have a limited frame of reference. God can do all things that are consonant with His nature. He can't tell a lie. He can't sin, even though He is omnipotent. God can also choose to limit the power He expresses. In light of the immense, complex, and powerful cosmos He has created, are we not presumptuous to ask what He is capable of?

THE TRINITY AND MATH

Here's another question that deals with God's nature, but on a more substantive level: How can God be three people and one at the same time?

For many critics and skeptics, the biblical idea of the Trinity—God the Father, God the Son, and God the Holy Spirit—is illogical. "Aha," they say, convinced they can prove our faith is out of the bounds of logic. "Three Gods do not make or equal one God. One plus one plus one does not equal one." They look at you with the same smug, confident glance as a boxer who has thrown a knockout blow. They wait for you to drop to your knees for the count of ten.

Is the idea of the Trinity really illogical? On the surface, of course, it seems to violate simple arithmetic, a most basic law of logic. Let's test it on a deeper level. Remember the law of noncontradiction that I wrote about in the last chapter? *"A"* cannot be *"A"* and *"non-A"* at the same time and in the same sense. This is a relevant test to apply to the idea of the Trinity. Christians do not believe, as cultists like the Jehovah's Witnesses try to make the naive think, that one God plus one God plus one God equals one God. The doctrine of the Trinity says there is in the one essence or substance of the deity three personalities: the Father, the Son, and the Holy Spirit, who exist at the same time forever. They are not three and one in the same sense. They are three persons but only one essence.

The doctrine of the Trinity, though a deep mystery, is not a contradiction. It does not violate the law of noncontradiction. It's reasonable and rational. One times one times one equals one.

The Bible certainly teaches there is one God. "Hear, O Israel: The LORD our God, the LORD is one!" (Deuteronomy 6:4). "There is one God," says Paul in 1 Timothy 2:5. "I am the LORD, and there is no other; there is no God besides Me" says the Holy Spirit through Isaiah (Isaiah 45:5a).

Though there is but one God, and we are monotheists and not tritheists (who believe in three Gods), the Bible clearly reveals the Father's personality, then it reveals the Son's personality, and then it reveals the Holy Spirit's personality. These three different personalities exist at the same time within the one essence of the Godhead.

The law of noncontradiction has not been violated, and our one God, in the forms of the Father, the Son, and the Holy Spirit, has not been proved unworthy of belief because of a fatal flaw of logic.

ATTRIBUTES MADE VISIBLE

How do we know what God looks like? The evidence of His characteristics—and even for His existence—are all around us. Why then do so many question who He is? Why do so many—even rather learned men, some with many degrees following their names—deny God exists? I believe the answer is found in Paul's epistle to the Romans:

> For the wrath of God is revealed from heaven against all ungodliness and unrighteousness of men, who suppress the truth in unrighteousness, because what may be known of God is manifest in them, for God has shown it to them. For since the creation of the world His invisible attributes are clearly seen, being understood by the things that are made, even His eternal power and Godhead, so that they are without excuse, because, although they knew God, they did not glorify Him as God, nor were thankful, but became futile in their thoughts, and their foolish hearts were darkened. Professing to be wise, they became fools, and changed the glory of the incorruptible God into an image made like corruptible man—and birds and four-footed animals and creeping things. (Romans 1:18–23)

It is not just from creation that we know about God. We know about Him from His revealed Word, the Bible, which we already have seen to be a reliable and trustworthy document. We know about Him through the life and teaching of His Son, Jesus Christ. Therein lies another problem for the skeptic. Lately, he and his fellow doubters have made it near fashionable to question not only the deity of Jesus, but also whether He actually existed.

Did Jesus Christ really live on planet Earth? Was He, as He claimed, the Son of God?

....

CHAPTER 6

Did Jesus Live?

*For we did not follow cunningly devised fables when we made known to you
the power and coming of our Lord Jesus Christ, but
were eyewitnesses of His majesty.*

2 PETER 1:16

I couldn't believe it. I thought I had heard it all.

Then one day a member of my congregation told me about a five-year-old neighbor who had just attended the first day of kindergarten in a public school. The teacher supposedly told the class, "No one can know for sure whether Jesus ever really lived." It's not clear whether the teacher actually said this or not, but what is clear is that the five-year-old was convinced Jesus' existence was in doubt—because the teacher said so.

Despite what some kindergarten teachers may say, Jesus Christ's historicity is well documented. We can reconstruct the highlights of Christ's life through non-Christian writers of the first century.[1]

"ISN'T JESUS JUST A MYTH?"

Sometimes otherwise intelligent people doubt that Jesus ever lived. Even though virtually no historians would deny Jesus' existence, these people are often heard asking, "Isn't Jesus just a myth?"

Second Peter 1:16 says Christians do not follow "cunningly devised fables." The word for "fable" here is the Greek word *muthos*, from which

"myth" is derived. A myth or fable is something existing only in the imagi-
nation, something that isn't historically true. By asking if Jesus is a myth,
people are staking claim to the possibility that He never existed.

Bertrand Russell, a famous philosopher of this century, often made
outrageous statements, without a shred of proof, that Jesus probably
didn't exist. Another recent skeptic of Jesus' existence is the atheist
Madalyn Murray O'Hair. Without any credentials—she is not a historian,
philosopher, or scholar—she publicly questioned whether Jesus lived.

So how do you deal with the question "Isn't Jesus a myth?" First, you
might want to go on the counteroffensive. "That's a very interesting
opinion," you might begin. "I suppose you know virtually no historian in
the world today would put his reputation on the line by stating that. The
evidence for Christ's existence is so overwhelming, they wouldn't dare
question it. Did you know that?"

BIBLICAL TESTIMONY

There is, first of all, the evidence of the Bible. The twenty-seven books of
the New Testament and a great deal of Old Testament prophecy (much of
which was fulfilled with Christ's first coming) speak powerfully and with
one voice about Jesus. Nowhere does the Bible say Jesus was a myth.

If the skeptic argues that the Bible can't be trusted, I hope you would
now be able to provide ample evidence, based on what you learned in the
first section of this book, of why the Bible is a credible, trustworthy, and
uniquely qualified book. In particular, you need to remember the law of
evidence introduced by the great law-and-evidence expert, Simon
Greenleaf: "Every document apparently ancient, coming from the proper
repository or custody, and bearing on its face no evident marks of forgery,
the law presumes to be genuine and devolves on the opposing party the
burden of proving it to be otherwise."[2] The Bible's testimony about Jesus is
certainly nothing to be dismissed.

Some, of course, would argue that the Bible is not objective in its
presentation of Jesus—that it is slanted by the writers, who were all

believers. Yet at the same time, these writers were recording history, what happened in that tumultuous first century. Isn't it interesting that we often accept other historians' writings without question, but if those historians happen to be Christian, they are somehow not as trustworthy.

These historians of the twenty-seven New Testament books are uniquely trustworthy. They have, in a sense, been cross-examined like no other historians in history. They have been cross-examined with the sword, torch, whip, heated iron, and cruel cross. They have been tortured as no other historian has ever been tortured before or since. Their testimony has stood the test. These men deserve our belief more than any historian who has never endured such a test of credibility.

Far from presenting Jesus as a mythical figure, the New Testament writers emphasized Jesus' flesh-and-bone existence. Frequently, they make mention that they were eyewitnesses of Christ. They listened to Him talk. They touched Him. They ate meals with Him. They knew Him well. He was by no means a myth to them.

Nonbiblical Testimony

The Bible is not the only testimony to Jesus Christ's having lived. You probably have heard someone say, "Well, after all, we don't know anything about Jesus except what we get in the Bible, and that's obviously unreliable." He or she may go on to claim that little or no evidence for Jesus comes from outside the Bible.

That simply is not true. There are, very clearly, at least nineteen early pagan writers who refer to Jesus Christ as an actual, real-life, historical figure: Tacitus, a great historian of Rome; Suetonius, also a historian; Pliny the Younger, one of the leaders of the Roman Empire; Epictetus; Lucian; Aristides; Galenus; Lampridius; Dio Cassius; Emeritus; Annianus (or Anianus); Marcellinus; Eunapius; and Zosimus. Some wrote entire works about Jesus, such as Lucian, Celsus (the first great antagonist, who wrote a whole book attacking Christianity), Porphyry, Hieracles, and Julian the Apostate.

Tacitus was the most famous of the Roman historians. Born in A.D. 55—in the middle of the New Testament period—he gives a thorough account of Christianity, which includes these facts:

- Christ, the founder of the Christian sect, was put to death as a malefactor by Pontius Pilate;
- Christianity began in Judea and spread in spite of Christ's ignominious death;
- Christianity encountered hatred and contempt throughout the Roman Empire, and vast multitudes of Christians were cruelly put to death in Rome at the hands of Nero as late as A.D. 64;
- The Jerusalem temple was destroyed, and the Jewish people were subjugated, which was a fulfillment of Christ's prophecy. (Josephus also wrote of these events.)

FURTHER TESTIMONY FROM PAGAN SOURCES

Pliny the Younger, a contemporary of Tacitus, wrote a letter to the emperor, Trajan, in A.D. 112. In his letter, Pliny expressed near panic. The spread of Christianity in Asia Minor, he reported, was happening at an astonishingly rapid rate among all ranks of society. He made mention of both the moral purity and the cruel persecution of these Christians. He also observed several of their beliefs, including their worship on the first day of the week and their adoration of Jesus Christ as God.[3]

Trajan, in his reply to Pliny's letter, remarked on the innocence of these Christians. He could see they were breaking no law, except in neglecting the worship of Roman gods, and he charged Pliny not to persecute these Christians.

Many writers don't take such a factual or just view of early Christians. Celsus, the first great anti-Christian writer, penned the second-century book *A True Discourse,* dismissing Christianity. A Greek philosopher, Celsus ruthlessly ridiculed the Christian faith. Using his considerable gifts of learning, philosophy, common sense, wit, sarcasm, and a dramatically animated style, he sought to disprove Christianity. Celsus combined a hatred of Judaism, contempt for heathenism, and an anticipation of most of the later deists' and naturalists' arguments.

Even Celsus, who despised Christianity, never considered claiming that Jesus Christ did not live. We can find no evidence, in fact, that anyone in the first few centuries after Christ even once questioned whether Jesus Christ was an actual, historical person. Only during the last few centuries, with the rise of modern skeptical philosophy, was the question first put forth that Jesus might be a myth.

RIDICULED BUT REAL

Celsus bears witness to the antiquity of the apostolic writings and furnishes strong arguments against modern mythical and legendary biographers of Jesus. Celsus refers to the Gospels of Matthew, Luke, and John and, in all, makes eighty allusions to quotations from the New Testament. Here are some of the particulars Celsus wrote about the Christian belief in Jesus Christ:

- He was born of a virgin in a small village of Judea;
- He was adored by wise men;
- His birth was followed by the slaughter of infants by order of Herod;
- He took flight to Egypt, where Celsus supposes Christ learned the charms of the magicians;
- After returning, He resided in Nazareth;
- He was baptized and the Holy Spirit descended on Him as a voice was heard from heaven;
- He elected disciples;
- He was a friend with publicans and other low people;
- He cured the lame and blind;
- He raised people from the dead;
- He was betrayed by Judas;
- He was denied by Peter.

In addition, Celsus refers to several details of Christ's passion, cruci-
fixion, and resurrection. Although he perverts and bends these historical
realities, he does regard them all as history. He does not, in any way, paint
Jesus Christ as a mythological figure. If Celsus were trying to disparage the
Christian faith, wouldn't it have been easy for him to write as Russell or
O'Hair would say in the twentieth century: "Ha, the whole thing is a myth.
Jesus never lived. We don't want to take any of it seriously"? Celsus, anti-
Christian as he was, knew he couldn't be intellectually credible and get
away with such a statement. Although he rejected the Christian faith, he
regarded Jesus Christ as a historical person.

JEWISH ACCOUNTS

Pagan writers weren't the only ones outside the Christian faith to acknowledge Christ's historical reality. Several Jewish writings also tell of His
flesh-and-blood existence. Both of the Gemaras of the Talmud refer to
Jesus. Although these consist of only a few brief, bitter passages intended
to discount Jesus' deity, these very early Jewish writings don't begin to hint
that He was not a historical person. According to the Gemara, Jesus:

- was the illegitimate son of Mary, whom they fancy was a hairdresser,
  and a man variously called Panthera;
- learned magical arts in Egypt, practiced them in Palestine, and
  therefore seduced and instigated the Israelites to rebellion;
- was crucified on the day preceding the Passover.

Of course, these are obvious perversions of the truths taught in the
Bible, but all these items and others are mentioned in both of the
Gemaras, the second part of the Jewish Talmud.

Flavius Josephus was the most highly reputed Jewish historian. Born
in A.D. 37, shortly after Christ's death, he wrote about the Jews' history and
wars. He also was a general in the Jewish army. In *The Antiquities of the
Jews*, book 18, chapter 3, section 3, he writes: "About this time lived Jesus,

a wise man, if it be proper to call him a man, for he was a doer of wonderful works, a teacher of such men as received the truth with pleasure. He drew over to him both many of the Jews and many of the Greeks. He was the Christ. And when Pilate, at the instigation of the principled men among us, had condemned him to the cross, those who had loved him at first, did not forsake him, for he appeared to them alive again on the third day, the divine prophets having foretold these and many other wonderful things concerning him. The sect of Christians so named after him are not extinct to this day."[4]

This passage is attacked viciously by skeptics. Why would Josephus, a general and a Jewish priest, ever write something like this? Therefore, they reason, it must be an interpolation, inserted into *The Antiquities of the Jews* by some Christian writer at a later date. Yet not a strand of evidence backs up this idea. Every single manuscript of *The Antiquities of the Jews*, without exception, contains that passage. Therefore, those who object to it can do so only based on their subjective and emotional hatred of what Josephus said.

The evidence is all on Christianity's side. Let's take a tally: twenty-seven books of the New Testament, nineteen pagan writers, and three Jewish writers testify to Jesus Christ's historical reality. Christians, indeed, did not follow a cunningly devised fable, but a real person. There were, as the Bible proclaims, eyewitnesses to His majesty. That historical fact is at the very foundation of the faith we hold.

So, when someone claims that Jesus was just a myth, don't panic. All you have to do is smile confidently, chuckle, and say, "You really aren't aware of the facts, are you? Let me enlighten you a little bit."

SEVERELY TESTED

One of the greatest historians of this century, Will Durant, is well respected by believers and unbelievers alike. To my knowledge, he was not a Christian. He wrote a classic, multivolume history of the world titled *The Story of Civilization*. In his third volume, *Caesar and Christ,* Durant

effectively puts the matter of Christ's historicity to rest: "The contradictions [in the gospels] are of minutiae, not substance; in essentials the
synoptic gospels agree remarkably well, and form a consistent portrait of
Christ. In the enthusiasm of its discoveries the Higher Criticism has
applied to the New Testament tests of authenticity so severe that by them
a hundred ancient worthies—e.g., Hammurabi, David, Socrates—would
fade into legend."[5]

In short, no scholar worthy of the name doubts whether Jesus of
Nazareth did indeed exist.

....

CHAPTER 7

Was Jesus God?

In the beginning was the Word, and the Word was with God, and the
Word was God. He was in the beginning with God. All things were made
through Him, and without Him nothing was made that was made.
In Him was life, and the life was the light of men. And the light shines in the
darkness, and the darkness did not comprehend it.

JOHN 1:1–5

I stood at the door, knocking. It was the home of a Jehovah's Witness. *A slightly different spin,* I thought to myself. I wondered how many times this had happened to them—to have a slightly obnoxious person on their porch.

I was a little upset; I wanted to get something straight. A woman who attends our church had told me that a Jehovah's Witness had visited her, and that the woman claimed she knew what John 1:1 meant in the original Greek—the verse that most Christians interpret, "And the Word was with God." The Jehovah's Witnesses will tell you, as did this woman, that there is no definite article in the Greek, and therefore it should be translated, "a god." Having studied Greek, I knew this to be untrue.

The woman opened the door. We began to talk, and soon we started to discuss Christ's deity. I told her, of course, that I believed Jesus Christ was God. She replied exactly how I expected her to—how, in fact, she had been trained to respond. "Oh, no, the Bible never teaches that," she said. I could see her lining up John 1:1 in her brain, ready to spring the trap.

I beat her to her own text. "Well, the Bible says, 'In the beginning was the Word, and the Word was with God, and the Word was God.'"

To which, of course, she said, "Oh, well, it doesn't say that in the Greek."

I looked at this woman with a sad smile. She likely had never studied Greek, and here she was telling people what the original Greek in the New Testament said. "Is that right?" I asked.

"Oh, yes, it doesn't say that in the Greek," she repeated, a little more forcibly.

"Well, I'm just amazed," I said to her. "I always thought it said 'En arche en ho logos, kai ho logos en pros ton theon, kai theos en ho logos.'"

Needless to say, she seemed a bit shocked. "What?"

"Well, I just happened to bring along my Greek New Testament, and I was hoping you could show me where my error in interpretation is. Could you do that for me?"

She took my Greek New Testament and, as God is my witness, she opened it up, looked at it and said, "What is this?"

"That's the Greek New Testament," I told her, "and you were going to show me where it says that Jesus isn't God."

"What is this?" she repeated.

"That is the Greek New Testament."

She turned it upside down, as if by staring at it from a new angle she might get some clue. "What is it?" she asked again.

"That is the Greek New Testament, and you were going to show me something in there."

Then—and I am not making this up—she turned it on its side and tried to read it that way. "What is this?"

"My dear lady, that is the New Testament in the original Greek language, and you were telling me what it said. I would like for you to show me where it says in the Greek that Jesus Christ was not God. You have been going all around the neighborhood telling people what the Greek New Testament says, so I just thought you might show me where it says that."

Well, she had no more knowledge of the Greek language than a fish does of the desert. She was simply parroting what she had been told. She might as well have been saying, "Polly wants a cracker." (Maybe they could teach her to say it in Greek.)

The Jehovah's Witnesses, as well as other cults, usually rely on indoctrination to pass along their religion. The reason is simple: If they let their people study God's Word as it really is, their whole movement would disintegrate. In fact, at the center of most cults that spring from Christianity is the central heresy that Jesus was not God.

The Jehovah's Witnesses even have a tract they hand out that says, "One plus one plus one equals three, not one." Therefore, Christians are illogical and contradictory when they believe in God the Father, God the Son, and God the Holy Spirit. Yet, as we have seen, a belief in the Trinity does not violate the law of noncontradiction: "A" cannot be "A" and "non-A" at the same time and in the same sense.

THE SON OF *WHOM?*

Still, the idea that Jesus is God has tripped up a number of people. The Pharisees' primary accusation of Jesus was that He had blasphemed by claiming to be God. Steeped in Deuteronomy 6:4—"Hear, O Israel: The LORD our God, the LORD is one"—most of the Jewish religious leaders couldn't imagine the possibility of a Son of God, let alone the Holy Spirit. Blasphemy was the official charge they placed on Jesus when they sought His execution.

The Pharisees, at the very least, had no doubts as to whether Jesus claimed to be God. That was the very thing that offended them. These pious Pharisees, then, are very different from many modern skeptics, for today it's chic to charge: "Well, after all, Jesus never claimed to be God."

There is a certain element of truth in this skeptical view. Jesus did not begin His ministry by claiming to be God. If you think about it, doesn't that make sense? Suppose Jesus, still wet from His baptism, walked into the temple and said, "I am the Messiah. I am your God. Fall down and worship Me." What do you think would have happened?

We would have had a premature crucifixion, and Jesus Christ would have had no ministry. All of His marvelous teaching would never have happened. Christ needed to start out by concealing, to some degree, His identity. He had to wait until the appropriate time, the time when His hour finally had come.

Yet even in the early part of His ministry, Christ did make some claims to divinity. When He was talking to the Samaritan woman at the well, His claim was direct. "The woman said to Him, 'I know that Messiah is coming' (who is called Christ). 'When He comes, He will tell us all things.' Jesus said to her, 'I who speak to you am He'" (John 4:25–26).

Now, that is about as clear-cut a statement as possibly could be made. So, why did He proclaim His identity to this woman? Think about it. Do you think she was going to have Him crucified? Was He in Jerusalem, where the scribes, Pharisees, and priests resided? No, He was in Samaria where neither a scribe nor a Pharisee would place one toe. That left Jesus free to make His messianic claim clear.

When Jesus was among the Jews, He both concealed and tantalized. They would, in fact, often ask, "Come out and tell us plainly: Are you or are you not the Christ?" Jesus would say something like, "I've already told you, and you didn't believe me." So He never would quite say. Not until the end of His ministry did Jesus make outright claims to the Jews that He, indeed, was the Son of God.

A GENTLEMAN OF THE STRICTEST ORDER

Yet in so many ways Jesus claimed divinity without spelling it out. At one time or another, for example, He claimed all the attributes of Deity:

Omnipresence

In Matthew 18:20, He said, "For where two or three are gathered together in My name, I am there in the midst of them." In Matthew 28:19–20, He states, "Go therefore and make disciples of all the nations...and lo, I am with you always, even to the end of the age." Many Christians have staked their lives on the trustworthiness of Christ's omnipresence. David Livingstone plunged into the deepest jungles of Africa on the promise of those verses. He said it was the word of a gentleman of the strictest order. It's even more than that; it's clearly a declaration of omnipresence. It's a statement of being God.

In Jesus' meeting with Nicodemus, He also claimed omnipresence. "No one has ascended to heaven but He who came down from heaven, that is, the Son of Man who is in heaven" (John 3:13). While talking to Nicodemus, Jesus was in Jerusalem, but He declared He was in heaven at the same time. So Christ clearly declared He was omnipresent.

Eternality

In John 6:62, Jesus says, "What then if you should see the Son of Man ascend where He was before?" He says in John 16:28, "I came forth from the Father and have come into the world. Again, I leave the world and go to the Father" and in John 17:5, "And now, O Father, glorify Me together with Yourself, with the glory which I had with You before the world was." These statements are clear claims of deity.

Omniscience

Several times, Jesus spoke of His ability to know everything. In Matthew 11:27b, He said, "No one knows the Son except the Father. Nor does anyone know the Father except the Son, and the one to whom the Son wills to reveal Him." In Revelation 2:23b, He said, "I am He who searches the minds and hearts." In Matthew 24:35, He was recorded as saying, "Heaven and earth will pass away, but My words will by no means pass away."

The Lord Jesus knows all things, including our hearts. Christ clearly claimed to have all knowledge, an attribute residing only in deity.

Omnipotence

In John 5:21, "For as the Father raises the dead and gives life to them, even so the Son gives life to whom He will." In John 10:30, He said, "I and My Father are one."

The Ruler of Angels

In Matthew 13:41, Jesus said, "The Son of Man shall send out His angels."

The Judge

In Matthew 25:31–32, 46, Jesus states, "When the Son of Man comes in His glory, and all the holy angels with Him, then He will sit upon the throne of His glory. All the nations will be gathered before Him, and He will separate them one from another.... And these will go away into everlasting punishment, but the righteous into eternal life." "For the Father judges no one, but has committed all judgment to the Son" (John 5:22).

According to these passages, the divine prerogative of judgment, which the Old Testament repeatedly declares to be God's, now belongs to God the Son. All nations will come before Him, and Christ will declare who goes to heaven and who goes to hell. If that is not a claim of deity, I don't know what is.

Allows Himself to be called God

In John 20:28, we read, "And Thomas answered and said to Him, 'My Lord and my God!'" As a Jew, Thomas is making a clear reference to Jesus as *the* Lord and *the* God. There is no mistaking his intention. (In the Greek, Thomas is calling Jesus "*the* Lord of me and *the* God of me.")

Forgiver of sins

The Old Testament made it clear that only God has the power to forgive sins. Yet Jesus claimed that power. Luke 7:48 records Jesus' response to a sinful woman. "Then He said to her, 'Your sins are forgiven.'" In Matthew 9:2 Jesus heals the paralytic: "Then behold, they brought to Him a paralytic lying on a bed. When Jesus saw their faith, He said to the paralytic, 'Son, be of good cheer; your sins are forgiven you.'" Clearly, the Jewish leaders knew Jesus was claiming the right of deity when He said He could forgive sins.

When Mark recounts this story, he writes, "Some of the scribes were sitting there and reasoning in their hearts, 'Why does this Man speak blasphemies like this? Who can forgive sins but God alone?'" (Mark 2:6–7). Again, in Matthew 9:3b–6, the religious leaders are aghast: "'This Man blasphemes!' But Jesus, knowing their thoughts, said '…Which is easier, to say, "Your sins are forgiven you," or to say, "Arise and walk"? But that you may know that the Son of Man has power on earth to forgive sins'; then He said to the paralytic, 'Arise, take up your bed, and go to your house.'"

Lord of the Sabbath

To the Jews, the Sabbath was very important. They were Sabbatarians of the strictest kind. Jesus, however, said, "For the Son of Man is Lord even of the Sabbath" (Matthew 12:8). It's incredible for anyone to claim he is Lord of any day: "I am the Lord of Tuesday," but Jesus declared He was Lord of the Sabbath, which until Christ's resurrection was the seventh day. Now, since then, it is the first day of the week.

Sinlessness

In Romans 3:23, the Bible clearly states that all men are sinners: "For all have sinned and fall short of the glory of God." Nonetheless, Jesus said in John 8:46, "Which of you convicts Me of sin?" Throughout the Bible, those who knew Him best concluded He was without sin.

Preexistence

In John 8:56–58, Jesus startled the Jews by another outrageous claim: "'Your father Abraham rejoiced to see My day, and he saw it and was glad.' Then the Jews said to Him, 'You are not yet fifty years old, and have You seen Abraham?' Jesus said to them, 'Most assuredly, I say to you, before Abraham was, I AM.'"

The Jews, of course, did not smile and say, "That's nice." Instead, they picked up stones to kill Him, which was the official Old Testament punishment for blasphemy. The Jews were quite familiar with God's identifying Himself to Moses as "I AM" (Exodus 3:14), and now, here was Jesus referring to Himself as I AM. The ruling Jews understood that He was claiming to be God.

When Jesus asked them for which good deed they were stoning Him, they replied, "For a good work we do not stone You, but for blasphemy, and because You, being a Man, make Yourself God" (John 10:33).

"Okay, I'm God"

Jesus, however, didn't always beat around the bush, making indirect claims of deity. Sometimes, especially near the end of His ministry, He came straight out and said, "Okay, I'm God." Although that is a bit of a paraphrase, Jesus clearly did state that He is the very manifestation of the Father. In John 14:9, He said: "Have I been with you so long, and yet you have not known Me, Philip? He who has seen Me has seen the Father."

What a statement! "If you have seen Me, you have seen God." Would you make a claim like that? Of course not. That is blasphemy or insanity, but Jesus declared it.

Jesus also claimed to be the Son of God even under oath. Listen to these claims. In John 5:25 He said, "Most assuredly, I say to you, the hour is coming, and now is, when the dead will hear the voice of the Son of God; and those who hear will live." While under oath and responding to the high priest, who asked, "'Are You the Christ, the Son of the Blessed?' Jesus said, 'I am'" (Mark 14:61–62a).

Keep in mind the stakes at this point. Jesus knew that if He said He was the Son of God, the Jews would understand He was claiming deity. That meant certain death. Yet under oath, Jesus said, "I am." That is as clear a claim of deity as you could possibly have.

He didn't leave it at that, however. He went on to say, "And you will see the Son of Man sitting at the right hand of the Power, and coming with the clouds of heaven" (Mark 14:62). Then again, "Do you say of Him whom the Father sanctified and sent into the world, 'You are blaspheming,' because I said, 'I am the Son of God'? If I do not do the works of My Father, do not believe Me" (John 10:36–37).

BOLSTERING HIS POSITION

Jesus Christ clearly claimed to be divine, and His position is offered considerable support by the remainder of the New Testament. Over and over again it states that Jesus is God. One of the central facts of the Bible is that Jesus is God. Scores of texts, both in Old Testament prophecy and in New Testament doctrine, proclaim His divinity. A few of the claims include:

- "For unto us a Child is born, unto us a Son is given [did you notice that a "child" is born, a "son" is given?].... And His name will be called Wonderful, Counselor, Mighty God" (Isaiah 9:6). This baby who would be born, the Son who is given, is the mighty God.
- "But you, Bethlehem Ephrathah, though you are little among the thousands of Judah, yet out of you shall come forth to Me the One to be Ruler in Israel, Whose goings forth are from of old, from everlasting" (Micah 5:2). This baby born in Bethlehem has existed and has been going forth from everlasting, from eternity.
- "In the beginning was the Word, and the Word was with God, and the Word was God.... All things were made through Him, and without Him nothing was made that was made" (John 1:1, 3).
- "And the Word became flesh and dwelt among us, and we beheld His glory, the glory as of the only begotten of the Father" (John 1:14).
- "For God so loved the world that He gave His only begotten Son, that whoever believes in Him should not perish but have everlasting life" (John 3:16).
- "And Thomas answered and said to Him, 'My Lord and my God!'" (John 20:28).
- "For in Him dwells all the fullness of the Godhead bodily" (Colossians 2:9). Jesus was the image of the invisible God. Have you

ever noticed the one divine attribute in the New Testament that is not attributed to Christ is invisibility? The Father is invisible; so the Son is the visible image of the Father.

• Lest we forget perhaps the most ringing endorsement of all, even God refers to Jesus as Son and as God, "But to the Son He [God] says, 'Your throne, O God, is forever and ever'" (Hebrews 1:8a). The Father calls the Son "God" in this verse.

THE EXCLAMATION POINT

Christ's resurrection serves as the exclamation point of His claim to divinity. In rising from the dead, He declared Himself the Son of God with power: "No one takes it [My life] from Me, but I lay it down of Myself. I have power to lay it down, and I have power to take it again" (John 10:18).

Jesus' claims to deity are overwhelming. Therefore, we must decide if He was crazy, or a deceiver, or telling the truth.

Was He a lunatic?

A liar?

Or, as He claimed, *Lord?*

C. S. Lewis, the great scholar and Christian writer, put it so well: "A man who was merely a man and said the sort of things Jesus said would not be a great moral teacher. He would either be a lunatic—on a level with the man who says he is a poached egg—or else he would be the Devil of Hell. You must make your choice. Either this man was, and is, the Son of God: or else a madman or something worse. You can shut Him up for a fool, you can spit at Him and kill Him as a demon; or you can fall at His feet and call Him Lord and God. But let us not come up with any patronising nonsense about His being a great human teacher. He has not left that open to us. He did not intend to."[1]

....

CHAPTER 8

Christ's Surprising Character Witnesses

"Behold, I make all things new."
REVELATION 21:5

Let's suppose you are on trial. The question put forth to the jury is simple: Has the defendant had a positive impact on the world?

As you sit behind the table, hoping that your five-hundred-dollar-an-hour lawyer is as good as he charges, you begin to sweat a little. Actually, a lot. In your mind, you start to stack up all your good little deeds: giving a one-hundred-dollar check to that starving little boy in Haiti—ahh, what was his name again? Or the time you told your wife she was lovely even though her hair looked liked Einstein's. What about that time when you saved that woman from drowning (at least you are pretty sure she wouldn't have made it to the shore).

As your mind races furiously, your lawyer winks at you, points to a group of scowling men and women, then whispers in your ear, "Here are your character witnesses." As your eyes move down the line of people, you gasp in horror. These people are your worst enemies!

There's Rick, whom you once called a jerk. Susan, whom you beat out of a promotion with some carefully placed words. Grant, who used to be your best friend, but whom you stopped seeing when he became such a whiner after his divorce. Oh no! There's your former boss, who thinks you were stealing office supplies from the company. Beside him is your former girlfriend, Allison, whom you dumped in tenth grade. (She went on to join a convent, but it doesn't look as if it has softened her attitude toward you any.) Sitting next to her is Nancy, the waitress at the D & D Diner, whom you stiff with your tip every lunch.

By now, the sweat is dripping off your forehead, running down your nose, and pooling on a pile of papers that your lawyer has sitting on the table. You begin to imagine how you would look in black-and-white stripes, going by the name "17938329." In a panic, you rise from your seat and scream at the judge, "Guilty! I'm guilty! Take me to my cell, sentence me to the electric chair. Just don't make me sit through this trial!"

The judge, who has been reading some official documents with his back to you, swivels in his chair at the sound of your outburst and looks at you. With horror, you realize it's your neighbor—the one whose dog you ran over with your car just last week.

The Enemies' Testimony

Can you imagine such a thing—being judged by your worst enemies? Well, in this chapter, that is what I propose to do. Not regarding your life, mind you, but Jesus Christ's. To show how great He was, I'm going to look at testimonies from some of His worst enemies through the last two thousand years: a rationalist philosopher, a couple of famous evolution-ists, a brilliant journalist, a world-renowned economist, a religious skeptic, and a famous science-fiction writer and Hollywood director. All of these men, mind you, were far from believers in Jesus Christ. In fact, most of them spent a good deal of their lives in active skepticism. Yet, amazingly, when you consider what they said about Jesus—His impact on history and the Bible's contributions to life—they tell a powerful story of a singularly great Person and a singularly great book.

As we have seen, some skeptics—and these are certainly farm-league skeptics—do not believe Jesus ever lived. Or, like Madalyn Murray O'Hair, they spend their lives vacillating between the idea that He never existed and the notion that yes, He did once live, but He was a terrible person who left a blight and a scourge on the world.

The greatest skeptics—at least the semihonest ones—have had enough sense to not only say Jesus lived, but also to acknowledge that He was the single greatest human being to walk the planet. Their verdict is unanimous: This One who was born in obscurity, who lived in poverty, and who died in agony, became the most important influence in the world, the greatest personage who ever lived. This One has influenced the world for good more than all of the philosophers and moralists combined.

AN IDEAL CHARACTER

Our first witness is William H. Lecky, one of the leading historians of the last century and author of *The History and Rise and Influence of the Spirit of Rationalism in Europe.* Clearly, this book was not a bastion of Christian dogma. Lecky spent his life advancing the cause of rationalism, attacking Christianity, and disbelieving Christ and the supernatural. Yet read what Lecky has to say about Christ and Christianity: "It was reserved for Christianity to present to the world an ideal character, which through all of the changes of eighteen centuries has inspired the hearts of men with an impassioned love, has shown itself capable of acting on all ages, nations, temperaments, and conditions, and has been not only the highest pattern of virtue, but also the strongest incentive to its practice, and has exercised so deep an influence that it may truly be said that the simple record of three short years of active life has done more to regenerate and soften mankind than all of the dispositions of philosophers and exhortations of moralists."[1]

This statement comes from the staunchest of unbelievers. Can you think of one of your enemies who would say something even sort of nice about you?

The testimonies of Jesus' foes go on and on. Actually, many of these people spent their younger and middle-age years excoriating the Bible and dismissing Jesus Christ. When they reached their more mature years, however, they reflected on what Christ has accomplished and became most vocal in their praise of Him.

John Stuart Mill is such a man. Perhaps the most influential and respected economist in the eighteenth century, he was considered by many to be one of the most brilliant men of history. Mill in his younger years often spoke with disdain about Christ, Christianity, and the Bible. Yet listen to what he believed about Jesus' character: "Christ is still left—a unique figure, not more unlike all of his precursors than all his followers, even those who had the direct benefit of his personal teaching. It is of no use to say that Christ, as exhibited in the Gospel, is not historical and that we know not how much of what is admirable has been added by the tradition of his followers.... Who among his disciples, or among their proselytes, was capable of inventing the sayings ascribed to Jesus or of imagining the life and character revealed in the Gospels? Certainly not the fishermen of Galilee."[2]

To this Mill adds: "When this preeminent genius is combined with the qualities of probably the greatest moral reformer and martyr to that mission who has ever existed on earth, religion cannot be said to have made a bad choice in pitching on this man as the ideal representative and guide of humanity; nor even now would it be easy, even for an unbeliever, to find a better translation of the rule of virtue from the abstract into the concrete than to endeavor to so live that Christ would approve our life."[3]

Mill never made the slightest profession of faith in Christ. In light of that, his words are puzzling. Yet they indicate how minds that are deep and powerful are forced at length to concede Jesus' greatness.

THEY FORGET

Or consider one of the most influential men to live in the last few centuries: Charles Darwin. Darwin, as you know, developed the theory of evolution, which has had an enormous impact on the way humans not only look at their origins, but also how they understand life and reality. Darwin once made a profession of faith in Christ, only later to abandon

Christianity completely. At one point, he made the statement that he could not understand how anyone could ever believe, or even imagine themselves to believe, in either Jesus Christ or the Bible.

Yet read the words he penned for a newspaper in London: "They forget or will not remember those who minimize the work of missionaries in pagan countries. They forget or will not remember that human sacrifices and the power of an idolatrous priesthood; a system of profligacy unparalleled in another part of the world; infanticide, a consequent of that system; bloody wars where conquerors spared neither women or children—that all of these have been abolished in these savage islands. And that dishonesty and temperance and licentiousness have been greatly reduced by Christianity. In a voyager, to forget these things is base ingratitude. For should he chance to be at the point of shipwreck on some unknown coast, he will most devoutly pray that the lesson of the missionary may have reached thus far."[4]

At another time, Darwin wrote: "The lesson of the missionary is the 'enchanter's wand.' The house has been built, the windows framed, the fields plowed, and even the trees grafted by the New Zealander. The march of improvement consequent on the introduction of Christianity throughout the seas probably stands by itself in the records of history."[5]

What an incredible statement from someone who believes in evolution, a theory that maintains humanity constantly is progressing toward greater and more wondrous things. Even with the passing of two thousand years, Darwin said there has yet to be a replacement for Jesus Christ's character.

SERIOUSLY PERPLEXED

Then there was Darwin's contemporary, his "bulldog" as it were, the man who did the most to popularize Darwin's theory: Thomas Huxley. As we saw earlier, Huxley was the first to coin the word *agnostic,* which is what he claimed to be. Huxley spent several years debating with bishops and theologians. He was opposed to most aspects of Christianity. Yet, writing in 1870 for the *Contemporary Review,* he penned these amazing words:

I have always been strongly in favor of secular education, in the sense of education without theology. But I must confess that I have been no less seriously perplexed to know by what practical measures the religious feeling, which is the essential basis of conduct, was to be kept up in the present utterly chaotic state of opinion on these matters without the use of the Bible. The pagan moralists lack life and color, take the Bible as a whole, make the severest deductions which bare criticism can dictate, and there still remains a vast residuum of moral beauty and grandeur. By the study of what other book could children be so much humanized and made to feel that each figure in that vast historical procession fills, like themselves, but a momentary space in the interval between two eternities and earns the blessing or curses of all time, according to its efforts to do good and evil?[6]

Huxley later chastised a fellow philosopher who debunked the Bible, telling the man he was putting on display his "conceited ignorance." (I guarantee that whatever you learned about Huxley in school, you didn't learn that.) Huxley went even further in his praise of the Bible: "The Bible has been the 'magna carta' of the poor and the oppressed down to modern times. No state has had a constitution in which the interest of the people are so largely taken into account, in which the duties so much more than the privileges of rulers are insisted upon as that drawn up for Israel. Nowhere is the fundamental truth that the welfare of this state in the long run depends upon the uprightness of the citizen so strongly laid down. I do not believe that the human race is yet and possibly never will be in a position to dispense with the Bible."[7]

Consider another voluble skeptic, George Romanes. He wrote many articles against Christianity during his lifetime. Shortly before his death, he reflected on matters moral and religious and wrote a book, which was published posthumously, titled *Thoughts on Religion*. Note Romanes's telling observation: "Not only is Christianity thus so immeasurably in advance of all other religions, it is no less so of every other system of thought that has ever been promulgated in regard to all that is moral and spiritual. Whether it be true or false, it is certain that neither philosophy, science, nor poetry has ever produced results in thought, conduct, or beauty in any degree to be compared with it. It is the greatest exhibition of the beautiful, the sublime, and all else that appeals to our spiritual nature which has ever been known upon our earth. What has all the science or all the philosophy of the world done for the thought of mankind to be compared with this one doctrine—God is love?"[8]

Christ's transformation of much of humanity has not escaped the notice of this skeptic.

A PENNILESS PREACHER

Moving into the twentieth century, let us consider one of the most famous historians, writers, and skeptics of the first half of this century—H. G. Wells, who wrote the famous *Outlines of History*. Probably best known for his science fiction and movie directing, he was, by profession, a historian as well as a very outspoken skeptic of Christianity. Wells, however, wrote these words about Jesus: "Jesus of Nazareth is easily the dominant figure in history. I am speaking of him, of course, as a man, for I can see that the historian must treat him as a man, just as the painter must paint him as a man. To assume that he never lived and that the accounts of his life are inventions is more difficult and raises more problems in the path of the historian than to accept the essential elements of the gospel stories as fact."[9]

He goes on: "Of course, you and I live in countries where to millions of men and women Jesus is more than a man. But the historian must disregard that fact. He must adhere to the evidence which would pass unchallenged if his book were to be read in every nation under the sun."[10]

Wells continues: "Now, it is interesting and significant, isn't it, that an historian, setting forth in that spirit without any theological bias whatsoever should find that he simply cannot portray the progress of humanity honestly without giving the foremost place to a penniless teacher from Nazareth."[11] This famous skeptic, as a historian, declares that Jesus Christ must be given the foremost place in the history of the human race.

STUPENDOUS SUCCESS

Further along in this century comes the brilliant and volatile journalist and writer, H. L. Mencken. It was Mencken who covered the Scopes trial for the *New York Times*. Even though the evolutionists lost in the courtroom, Mencken's writings led to a victory in the court of public opinion. In writing about the trial, Mencken dipped his pen in acid when it came to discussing Christians and Christianity. Yet in 1930 when he wrote a work entitled "Treatise on the Gods," Mencken said this:

> This historicity of Jesus is no longer questioned seriously by anyone, whether Christian or unbeliever. So when I tell you it's not questioned by historians and skeptics, here is a famous skeptic telling you that it is no longer questioned seriously by anyone, whether Christian or unbeliever. The main facts about Him seem to be beyond dispute....
>
> It is not easy, to account for his singular and stupendous success. How did it come about that one who in his life had only the bitter cup of contumely to drink should have lifted himself in death to such vast esteem and circumstance, such incomparable and world-shaking power and renown. Unless the whole New Testament is to be rejected as moonshine. It seems to be certain that many persons saw him after his supposed death on the cross, including not a few who were violently disinclined to believe in his resurrection. Upon that theory, the most civilized section of the human race has erected a structure of ideas and practices so vast in scope and so powerful in effect that the whole range of history shows nothing parallel.[12]

When other skeptics remonstrated with Mencken about his comments, he refused to withdraw them or to edit them in future editions.

Jesus Christ. He claimed to be God.

Lunatic? He was the most credible, balanced person who ever lived.

Liar? His was the most noble life ever lived on the planet.

If you don't believe me, just ask His worst enemies.

PART THREE

Answers to Common Objections

....

CHAPTER 9

Is Jesus the Only Way?

Jesus answered, "I am the way and the truth and the life.
No one comes to the Father except through me."
JOHN 14:6, NIV

D r. R. C. Sproul, one of the greatest contemporary theologians and apologists, was on the hot spot. Part of the problem was that he wasn't Dr. Sproul but rather just R. C. Sproul, a lowly freshman in college. Another part of the problem was that he was a relatively new convert to Christianity, with neither a deep understanding of his faith nor the ability to defend it. Most of the problem was that he was being ridiculed by an angry, militant, anti-Christian professor.

Sproul was sitting innocently enough in his freshman college English class. Perhaps he was daydreaming. Right in the middle of class, the professor—a former war correspondent hostile to Christianity—looked at R. C. and asked, "Mr. Sproul, do you believe that Jesus Christ is the only way to God?" Now, what this had to do with Shakespeare, Joyce, T. S. Eliot, or any other great writer of English literature is anybody's guess, but there it was—a hand grenade tossed into Sproul's lap.

R. C. was shaken by the question. "I gasped," he said of the moment, which he believes to be one of the most humiliating in his life. "I felt the weight of her question, and I knew that every eye in the room was on me. My mind raced for a way to escape my dilemma. I knew if I said yes, people would be angry. At the same time, if I said no, I would be betraying Christ."

Sproul muttered almost inaudibly, "Yes, I do."

The teacher responded with unmitigated fury. In front of the class, with a voice as loud as a rocket launcher, she yelled at Sproul, "That is the most narrow-minded, bigoted, and arrogant statement I have ever heard in my life! You must be a supreme egotist to believe that your way of religion is the only way."

Sproul, thoroughly embarrassed and taken aback, slouched meekly in his chair without saying another word.

Even the great ones like R. C. Sproul have failed to defend Christianity. As Sproul grew as a Christian, he learned how to be an effective spokesman for the faith. (If he were back in that classroom now, he would have that professor for lunch and still have room for dessert!) I share this story to encourage you. Even if you may have failed in the past, you also can become better prepared to give "a ready defense" for your Christian faith.

The Cultural Climate: "Tolerance" and "Intolerance"

The professor's charge is one with which you will have to learn to deal. The question will come in various forms: "Well, all religions are the same, so why insist that yours is the only right one?" or "Why would you be so narrow-minded as to believe Jesus is the only way to God? Isn't that the height of bigotry?" Whatever the form, this question is always embedded in the idea of tolerance.

If the moral and cultural climate of our age has any theme, it is that of tolerance. To an immoral, ungodly, and sinful generation, the only virtue that remains is tolerance of everybody else's sin. Therefore, the only vice that remains is intolerance. That is precisely what you have. It's a matter of wickedness protecting its own turf under the guise of tolerance.

Do you notice something peculiar about this tolerance? As with Sproul's professor, tolerance goes only so far. It seems to come to a screeching halt right at the door of Christianity. Christians who stand up for what they believe are accused of intolerance, yet those making the accusation are themselves displaying incredible intolerance of Christian belief.

If you find yourself in a situation similar to that of Sproul in his freshman English class, you might try responding this way: "Now, why would you say a thing like that? Why would you so viciously and publicly attack me for the views I hold, which don't happen to be the views you hold? Are you so bigoted and intolerant yourself? I haven't attacked you or your view. You are the one who has attacked me. It seems to me that that is an egotistical, bigoted, intolerant attitude on your part."

The hypocrisy of another's own intolerance leads us to examine just what tolerance is. Is it really egotistical to believe Christianity is the only true religion? No. The only way something can be egotistical is if someone maintains it's true only because it happens to be what *he* believes. If he believed something else—something that was the exact opposite—then *that* would be the truth...to him! In other words, a precept's truthfulness is derived solely from one's decision to believe it. *That's* egotistical.

What if I believe Jesus Christ is the divine Son of God—in fact, God incarnate, because He has said, as we saw at the opening of this chapter, "I am the way and the truth and the life. No one comes to the Father except through me" (John 14:6, NIV)? Such being the case, I would like to pose another question for that professor as well as the other disciples of tolerance. "Ma'am, would you say that Jesus Christ was a bigot?"

I think she would feel she were on the horns of a dilemma at that point. If believing that Christ is the only way is an example of bigotry and intolerance, then Jesus Christ is evidently an intolerant bigot.

THE GOOD SIDE OF DISCRIMINATION

The idea of tolerance, as it's generally defined in today's culture, is neither biblical nor logical. The Bible clearly teaches that we should not tolerate all things. It tells us that we should hate evil and that we should be discriminating. I'm sure the media would love to get hold of that, so please listen carefully. God's Word tells us that we should discriminate, not between colors of skin, but between that which is good and that which is evil.

One of our time's problems is that people say they accept everything. You can't accept God and the devil. What place has Christ with Belial, the devil? You can't accept all things.

In fact, one of the tests of maturity is the ability to discern between that which is morally good and that which is morally evil and to choose the one and reject the other. Tolerance is not the only virtue.

Tolerance, of course, is a natural and valuable part of the American experience. On our coins and in our minds is stamped *e pluribus unum,* which means "out of many, one." This is an important reality—out of the many peoples who have made this country home, there is one America, the so-called melting pot. Unfortunately, the melting pot seems to have melted down, and we are becoming more and more divided.

This is also true of our religious experience. Our forefathers, themselves the victims of religious intolerance, took great pains to ensure freedom of religion. The idea is at the heart of this country. Along with many nationalities and races, there would be many religions also. The American spirit's essence is that we should be tolerant of other people—of their nationalities, of their race, and of their religions. I wholeheartedly agree with that. Far too much intolerance in those areas is expressed in our world, nation, and even church.

TOLERANCE EQUALS EQUALITY?

From the idea of tolerance has sprung the false concept of equality. Since all religions are to be tolerated, then they must be equally valid. If they are equally valid, they must be equally good and true. It is here that we have reached the deadly quicksand of distortion.

To illustrate, I turn to Sproul once again—and in a more positive light! Years later, instead of an angry, militant professor, Sproul encountered a

Baha'i priest in a public forum. Now, you're probably not very familiar with the religion of Baha'i—it's not in the top ten of the world's religions, but it is, nevertheless, a religion. It's also a bastion for tolerance. In a sort of United Nations approach to faith, the Baha'is believe in just about everyone. Jesus Christ is placed as a peer with all of the rest—Buddha, Lao-tzu, Confucius, Mohammed, Zoroaster, etc. They are all the same. Baha'i picks up on the spirit of the age and formalizes it into a religion.

This time Sproul was prepared. This is a short synopsis of what he said to the Baha'i priest:

How can you believe that all religions are essentially the same when so many of these religions contradict each other? For example, Christianity says that Christ came so people could have life, have it more abundantly and have it eternally. Buddhism and Hinduism, on the other hand, teach that life is a great evil. What we should seek after is the ending of all personal life in nirvana, where the individual drop of water, as an individual life, falls back into the ocean and all conscious existence ceases. This is what Buddhism and Hinduism offer to humanity—the cessation of personal consciousness. Life is perceived to be miserable (paganism always makes life miserable). Both Hinduism and its reformed aspect of Buddhism, which is sort of a Protestant version of Hinduism, teach the same thing—the cessation of life. Christ, however, teaches eternal life in paradise. Are those the same thing?

Islam, or Mohammedanism, as it is sometimes incorrectly called, vigorously teaches that there is one God. Hinduism, on the other hand, teaches that there are at least 300 million gods. Question: Are those the same thing?

Confucianism recognizes no god. Are those the same thing?

You, sir, are you really telling me all religions are the same? I suggest you go home and learn something about a religion before you talk about it, because nothing could possibly be further from the truth than that.

AN AUDACIOUS ANSWER

So far, so good. A rational debate had just begun. What the Baha'i priest said in response to Sproul was simply astonishing. "I don't know anything about Islam, Buddhism, Hinduism, or Confucianism. I just believe all religions are the same."

Do you understand what this priest was doing? He had the audacity to get up and tell people, without knowing anything about such things, that all religions are the same. Incredible.

Yet most of the disciples of tolerance in our culture are equally ignorant. Whenever you hear someone say all religions are basically the same, you can safely assume the person you are talking to is ignorant. He or she doesn't know anything about religions. Anyone who has made a serious study of the world's religions would never claim they are all the same.

When discussing the concept of "equally true," we must return to the law of noncontradiction that we examined earlier. If you will recall, this fundamental law of logic states that "A" cannot be "A" and "non-A" at the same time and in the same sense. So, if one religion teaches that life is something to be lived abundantly and another religion teaches that life is something to be escaped from, then "A" has already contradicted itself. Life cannot be two different things at the same time and in the same sense. Truth, by its very definition, cannot be all-inclusive. For something to be true, there must be this corresponding reality: Some things, therefore, are not true.

Scripture clearly teaches that all religions are not equally good and equally true. In 1 Corinthians 10:20, the apostle Paul wrote, "The things which the Gentiles sacrifice they sacrifice to demons and not to God, and I do not want you to have fellowship with demons." This is a very sobering text. It states that God chose to reveal His Savior and His way of salvation through the Hebrew people. The rest of the world went out into pagan darkness and worshiped false gods, which were demons. That is an awesome concept, totally foreign to the *Zeitgeist* of this age—but it's what the Bible says.

As Christians, we must not go to the other extreme and also violate the law of noncontradiction by saying, "If Christianity is the only true religion, then all the other religions are completely false." Don't ever make that blunder of logic. Most religions teach that murder, theft, and rape are wrong. Those things are self-evidently true.

GOLD OR SILVER?

Religious similarities are not as many as the disciples of tolerance would like to claim. Most people who preach tolerance would say all religions teach the Golden Rule, for example. That is simply not true. No religion teaches the Golden Rule but Christianity. Now, many other religions teach what I would call the "silver rule." Buddha taught it: "All things you would that men do not unto you, do not unto others." That is the silver rule. It's stated in the negative.

What Jesus taught, the Golden Rule, is vastly more difficult. "Therefore, whatever you want men to do to you, do also to them" (Matthew 7:12). You're in a different ballpark altogether. It's like the difference between a sandlot field, with rags for bases, and Yankee Stadium.

The differences between religions, however, are usually not so subtle. The Bible believes man is sinful and depraved. Confucius believed man was basically good. He didn't know anything about heaven. He didn't believe in God. Are those religions the same?

There is an even greater difference between Christianity and other religions. It's a fundamental and critical distinction: Ethical teachings are not the essence of Christianity. Even Christ's teachings, great as they were, are not numbered among the church's core beliefs. That is different from every other religion.

TRUTH IS A PERSON

Here is the critical distinction: Truth is not just something you believe or something you do, but rather it's a person—Jesus Christ. "I am the truth," Jesus said. He didn't choose to say, "I speak the truth," or "I know the truth," or "I will give you the truth," but "I am the truth." That changes everything.

Many religions rely on an external following of the truth—obeying commands or chanting mantras or practicing love—to achieve some elevated level of being, increased consciousness, goodness, or heaven. They teach that the truth is something that works externally.

The Bible, however, teaches that truth is a person, not a thing. Truth is a matter of internal incarnation—that Jesus, the truth, lives inside each born-again Christian. Truth is not primarily something we do but a person who lives inside us, breaking out into reality in acts of love. When Jesus said, "I am the truth and the truth will set you free," He was speaking of the incarnational reality of truth. The truth is that God sent His Son to this strange planet to die for our sins so that we, who were absolutely helpless, might have eternal life.

That is why the center of Christian belief is not a list of rules to be followed but a person to be experienced. That core of Christianity is:

- Christ, conceived of a virgin
- Christ, the Son of God
- Christ crucified, suffering the punishment for sin and the wrath of God
- Christ resurrected by God into new life
- By Christ, the gift of eternal life for everyone who believes in Him

A MARKED DIFFERENCE

No moral code or ethical teaching is to be found in that list of essentials. This is vastly different from any other religion. Other religions are based on their founders' teachings; Christianity is based on its Founder's life. If

Gautama Buddha had never lived, you could still have Buddhism. In fact, Mary Baker Eddy taught a Westernized version of it. Buddhism is simply a matter of teachings. Anybody could have come up with it at any place, at any time. If Jesus Christ had never existed, however, there could be no Christianity. These religions are not the same thing.

Christianity's core beliefs have nothing to say about His teaching, His preaching, His example, His commandments—none of those things— because Christianity does not rest on Christ's teachings. It rests on His person, His birth, His atoning death, and His resurrection. What are the great festivals of the Christian faith? Christmas, Good Friday, and Easter; birth, death, and resurrection.

Birth: The incarnation of God in human flesh is celebrated at Christmas. That's taught by no other religion.

Death: The atoning death of the Son of God for the sins of the world is observed at Easter. That's not taught (much less accomplished) by any other religion.

Resurrection: In the words of Christ, "I am He who lives, and was dead, and behold, I am alive forevermore (Revelation 1:18), and "Because I live, you [who trust in Me] will live also" (John 14:19).

Did any other religious leader claim to be the truth? Did Confucius die for the sins of the world? No, he didn't even believe in sin. Did Mohammed die for the sins of anybody? Did Buddha, Lao-tzu, Zoroaster? Absolutely none of them. Only Christ is a Savior who died an atoning death for the sins of the world.

Only Christ rose from the dead. Buddha, Mohammed, Confucius, and all the rest died, and they haven't been heard from since. Jesus Christ's resurrection is unique.

Shrink Back No More

So the next time you hear someone say, "Oh, all religions are the same," don't do what that young R. C. Sproul did in his freshman English class. Don't shrink back from the truth. Not all religions are the same. Christ and

Christianity are uniquely and fundamentally different. All other religions, if they offer salvation at all, are based on good works. Jesus Christ, by His work on the cross, has set His followers free from the impossible feat of earning their salvation. In Christianity, salvation is a free gift. Confucius didn't believe in salvation. He said, "We don't even know anything about life, much less anything about death." Is that the same? Not at all.

Someone once made this analogy: All humanity is drowning, and the religions of the world are like a lifeguard throwing humanity a set of instructions on how to swim (how to save himself). Christianity is akin to the Savior Himself jumping into the water to save humanity at the expense of His own life.

When Christians say Jesus is the only way to God, we are not being bigoted or intolerant. We simply are quoting Jesus Christ Himself, for He is the one who said, "I am the way, the truth, and the life. No one comes to the Father except through Me" (John 14:6).

Nobody made that up. It's straight from the mouth of God the Son.

....

CHAPTER 10

What about the Problem of Evil?

"When I looked for good, evil came to me; and when I waited for light, then came darkness."
JOB 30:26

The doctor, serving God in a hospital in a remote part of Haiti, was puzzled by the name of a little girl who had been brought in for treatment. Her name was Assez-dents, which roughly translated means "enough teeth." What an odd name.

The doctor asked the girl's father, a raggedly dressed man from one of the isolated peasant regions, why he chose the name.

The man smiled and said, "It was a name that was there."

The doctor probed further. The father had had eight children. Seven had already died. After further investigation, the doctor concluded the name came directly from the man's religion, which happened to be voodoo.

Figuratively, "enough teeth" meant "enough of this suffering and death" or, in a purely voodoo sense, "enough of these spirits who are eating my children."

The name is very revealing, not only of a father's heart cry for the destruction to come to an end, but also of profound truth: What you believe about God (or the gods) affects how you view and live life. At voodoo's core, for instance, is the belief that everything happens because of a spiritual cause. That is, the spirits fix the results. Planted deeply in many a Haitian mind is the thought that God is responsible for both good and evil. He is capable of helping, but He is also capable of playing nasty, even deadly, tricks. Underneath God are complex layers of intermediary deities, with certain predefined powers and territories, who mostly do evil. Below this level are a few humans who have acquired the skill to petition the gods. People come to these religious mediums to ask the gods to do as they are bid. These mediums are the magicians, sorcerers, and witch doctors. In Haiti, they are known as the *bokor.*

Getting ahead in life to most Haitians means successfully bribing the gods. It means countering the gods who have been petitioned to do you harm. It's a cycle of spells, potions, and charms that builds on itself. In the end, the cycle leads to a sense of powerlessness, fatalism, and paradoxically, to a hunger for revenge. It's a terrible way to live.

What you believe about God and His relation to good and evil will, without question, color the way you live in the world. In fact, history is a long procession of gods who not only allowed evil but also were the source of it. The Roman and Greek gods, for example, were not much better than the voodoo gods. They were merely men, with all of their sins and foibles, writ large. They could wake up with a headache and wreak havoc on any nation or individual.

The problem of evil wasn't discussed by the Greek or Roman philosophers for a simple reason: All they had for gods was Zeus and his family, which comprised the Greek pantheon, and, with different names, the Roman pantheon of gods. These gods were all sinful beings or worse. Many of the so-called gods were demons.

If you were to go to India and enter the temples to examine the idols, you would see they are demonic. The apostle Paul was right when he said that those who worship idols are worshiping demons. What a horrible prospect—to think of a god as evil.

What if God were omniscient, omnipotent, and bent on evil? Ponder, my friend, what it would be like to know God had all the malice and hatred of Satan yet also had absolute power and knowledge. That, indeed, would be enough to make you tremble.

When the world became aware of the Hebrew concept of God, people were puzzled. Up to that point, God had not been a holy, just, and good god, but rather one like in voodoo, capable of both good *and* evil. No one blamed God for allowing evil to happen but simply counted Him as one of those responsible for evil. That was just the way it was. With the introduction of a purely good God, which was the Hebrew concept, the dichotomy of God and evil became a pressing question.

With the advent of Christianity came the first *theodicy*, which in the Greek means "God" and "justice." A theodicy is a defense of God's justice in light of evil's presence in the world. It is, in comparison with other possibilities, a rather good problem to have.

We proclaim, by Scripture's authority, that our God—the Judeo-Christian God—is good, holy, and loving. In that context—and only in that context—the question springs up: How can a good God allow evil? Or, even more difficult, and one of the favorite questions of skeptics: Why has so much evil happened in the name of God?

NOMINAL VS. TRUE CHRISTIANITY

The question of evil in God's name takes many forms. One of the most common is, What about the Crusades? Didn't Christians do endless evil in God's name? What about the Inquisition?

One of the first things we must examine is whether the Christians involved were true Christians or nominal Christians, which means Christians in name only. Christ made it clear that some individuals are truly part of His church—what is called the invisible church—which is made up of all of God's elect, all of those who are regenerated by His Spirit and have been sanctified and justified. This invisible church exists in the larger, visible church. Not all of those in the larger, visible church are members of the invisible, true church.

Using a metaphor, Christ predicted tares among the wheat and goats among the sheep. The tares and goats are really false believers. Even among the twelve apostles there was the apostate Judas, who was never a member of the true church. Early on Jesus said, "Have not I chosen you twelve, and one of you is a devil," not a saint (John 6:70, KJV). Many claim to be Christians, but they aren't really at all.

Unfortunately, the nominal Christian has never truly given his heart and life to Jesus Christ. He is not a "new creature," as described in 2 Corinthians 5:17 (KJV). His spirit has not been born again, so he does not experience Christ's transforming power. He is still the same ol' person with all the capabilities for evil that the worst pagan has, and yet he bears the name "Christian." Thus he is able to do an enormous amount of damage to the church and to the cause of Christ. So many of the evils attributed to Christians are committed by nominal Christians.

We have a contemporary example of this in the fighting in Ireland, which in reality is mostly political. It is between a Roman Catholic and a Protestant group, at least in name. I asked several Irish Protestant ministers, who were in the heart of all this, "How is it you allow Christians to fight and kill others?"

"What do you mean 'Christians'?" they all asked me.

"Well, the Protestants right there in the midst of that."

"Those people aren't Christians," was the answer they gave me. "They are nominal Christians. They never darken the doors of our churches."

It's like the difference between a government-issued hundred-dollar bill and a counterfeit hundred-dollar bill. One of the bills has the backing of the government and is recognized as legitimate. The other is an imitation of the genuine bill, and the government doesn't recognize it. Just because someone calls himself or herself a Christian doesn't make it so, any more than calling a counterfeit bill legitimate makes it so.

BACK TO THE CRUSADES

Which brings us back to how we should answer the question about the evil done in God's name during the Crusades. First, let's put the Crusades in their historical perspective. Our response to the questioner is to ask, "Which Crusade do you have in mind?"

You see, the First Crusade was really undertaken by the Muslims when they captured the Holy Land along with all of Christianity's sacred places. Jerusalem fell to the Muslim hordes under Caliph Omar in A.D. 637, exactly fifteen years after the beginning of Islam or the Mohammedan faith. The Muslims traveled with the scimitar (the sword), and in many cases, they gave people only two choices: convert or die. The "infidels," as the Muslims were called, captured the Holy Land; Bethlehem, the place of Christ's birth; Galilee, where He ministered; Calvary, where He suffered and died; and the Holy Sepulchre, where He was buried and from which He rose. Over the years, some thirty thousand Christian churches or other Christian buildings in that area were destroyed by the Muslims or were converted into mosques. When the order went out to destroy the church of the Holy Sepulchre, Christians in Europe reacted by organizing their own Crusade—the Second Crusade, really—to reclaim Christianity's holy places.

Don't get me wrong; I am not defending the Crusades. Many terrible things were done on both sides, but isn't it interesting that we never hear something like this: "General Douglas MacArthur and the Allied Forces held a crusade against the Philippines and invaded those islands, driving out the people. Many thousands of lives were lost, and much property was destroyed. Terrible, terrible, terrible. He even said he was going to do it when he announced, 'I shall return.' Remember that?"

The story about the Philippines makes a lot more sense when put into perspective. The Japanese, who were driven out of those islands, had themselves invaded and conquered that land some years before. The United States and the other allies restored the Philippines to their proper owners.

Again, I do not defend the Crusades, but it is only intellectually honest to place them in their historical context. The Christian Crusade was, in historical fact, a response to the Muslim Crusade, but how many times do you ever hear anyone talking about the Muslim Crusade? A little balance is needed for clearer understanding.

What about the Inquisition?

A second incarnation of the question about the coexistence of God and evil is "What about the Inquisition?"

Again, some historical context is needed. The Spanish Inquisition began in the year A.D. 1233. The Protestant Reformation had not yet taken place—that was still some three hundred years in the future. So we, as Protestants, had no part in the Inquisition. We were not even around at that time. When Protestantism did come into existence, you have to understand that evangelical Protestants often were on the receiving end of the Inquisition, tortured and killed for their beliefs. None were on the giving end. To blame real Christians for the Inquisition is an utter distortion. We were not involved, except as victims.

What about the Holocaust?

A third question about evil is stated something like this: "Oh, Christianity, look at what you have done. There is the Holocaust. Adolf Hitler was a Christian, and you know what he did to the Jews."

This perspective is widely held, especially among Jews. Many are under the impression that Hitler was a Christian, which, in fact, is not true. Although Hitler was born and raised a Roman Catholic, he abandoned that faith very early in his life. He described himself as "a total pagan." He furthermore said that the kaiser had failed because he was a Protestant. "But I will succeed because I know about this Roman Catholic thing, and I know how to control it," he said.

In fact, Hitler had plans to destroy Christianity, which he considered the illegitimate offspring of Judaism. Once he extirpated the Jews, whom he described as "human bacteria," he would kill Christians, which he had already begun to do. The Holocaust involved the murdering of eleven to sixteen million people. Six million of these individuals were Jews. Most of the rest were Christians—real and nominal. Dr. David Barrett points out that one-sixth of all the Jews killed in the Holocaust were also professing Christians (that is, they were baptized or were converts in some other way).[1]

Hitler was a pagan. If he had any religion, he believed in the ancient German pagan gods, and he wanted to restore that virile religion, which took life without compassion or concern and was emboldened to do anything it wanted. He looked upon the "God of the deserts" (his derisive description of the Judeo-Christian God) as a god who had brought man into servility.[2] William Shirer, a journalist who covered the Nazi regime and wrote the widely respected book *The Rise and Fall of the Third Reich,* said, "The Nazi regime intended eventually to destroy Christianity in Germany, if it could, and substitute the old paganism of the early Germanic gods and the new paganism of the Nazi extremists."[3]

Hitler was also an ardent follower of Friedrich Wilhelm Nietzsche, who was an atheist and the original founder of the "God is dead" movement. Nietzsche believed in the "super man" who would eventually become god. It was from this concept that Hitler derived his idea of the "super race," the Nazi Aryan race, which was destined to rule the world. He declared, "The heaviest blow that ever struck humanity was the coming of Christianity. Bolshevism is Christianity's illegitimate child. Both are inventions of the Jew."[4]

No, Hitler was not Christian. Neither was the Holocaust.

WHAT ABOUT RELIGIOUS WARS?

A fourth question, which is closely tied to the first three, is "How many people have died in wars fought in the name of religion?" The common belief is that more people have died in the name of religion than in all other wars put together.

This is pure nonsense. In fact, most of the wars in recent history have been at the instigation of atheistic states. Hitler killed 11 to 16 million people, not to mention the millions who died in the war. Joseph Stalin, another anti-Christian, killed 40 million people. By the way, Stalin was raised Russian Orthodox. He studied for the priesthood, but he utterly apostatized, hating Christianity and God and closing 90 percent of the churches in the Soviet Union. Hitler has killed his millions; Stalin has killed his tens of millions. Mao Tse-tung, however, is the grand winner— or loser—with estimates that he killed 72 million people.

All in all, the Communists alone, who are atheists by constitution, are responsible for murdering 130 million people, and that isn't counting those killed in war. In this century alone, at the hands of ungodly pagan states, about 170 million people have been killed. The Inquisition involved about 12,000 people in Spain and 30,000 people altogether.

The idea that more people have died because of religious wars than anything else is utterly fallacious. More people have been killed in the twentieth century alone by atheistic states than in all other wars—religious and otherwise. Christians are on far more solid ground than most people realize—rock solid. We don't need to shrink back in embarrassment over historically incorrect assertions regarding God's relation to evil.

CAN A LOVING GOD CONDEMN INNOCENT PEOPLE TO HELL?

A far larger question that explores the relationship between God and evil is "How can a loving God send people to hell?" This question is often even more focused, "Do you mean to tell me God is going to send some poor person in Africa or Asia or China to hell for simply not believing in a Christ he never heard of?"

My short answer would be: No, I don't believe God is going to send people to hell for their ignorance. Notice I didn't say, "No, I don't believe they are going to hell." The Bible makes it clear that, when it comes to God, no one is ignorant. Romans 1:19–21 states: "Because what may be known of God is manifest in them, for God has shown it to them. For since the creation of the world His invisible attributes are clearly seen, being understood by the things that are made, even His eternal power and Godhead, so that they are without excuse, because, although they knew

God, they did not glorify Him as God, nor were thankful, but became futile in their thoughts, and their foolish hearts were darkened."

God has revealed by His creation that a divine Person created this world, and everywhere among all of the tribes of the world exists a belief in a God who is a Creator. It's only in the twentieth century, the century of atheism, through the sophisticated and cunning philosophies of evolution and communism, that people have been twisted into disbelieving in God and believing in those ideologies instead.

God has revealed Himself to all of humanity in several ways. The first is the light of *creation*: "For since the creation of the world His invisible attributes are clearly seen, being understood" (Romans 1:20). The psalmist tells us, "The heavens declare the glory of God; and the firmament shows His handiwork. Day unto day utters speech, and night unto night reveals knowledge. There is no speech nor language where their voice is not heard" (Psalm 19:1–3). The stars in the heavens, the sun, and the moon declare that the hand that made them is divine and that this is known everywhere.

God also has revealed Himself in the light of *conscience*. Romans 2 says that individuals' consciences will accuse or excuse them in the day when God will judge their secrets. Everyone has been given a moral monitor that tells him or her that some things are right and some things are wrong. Even though people attempt to sear their consciences by immoral and ungodly living, they are responsible. No one is able to completely sear his or her conscience.

As a result, no one can claim ignorance. No one can say that because he never read the Ten Commandments he isn't guilty. The law is written on everyone's conscience. Paul states, "Therefore you are inexcusable, O man, whoever you are who judge, for in whatever you judge another you condemn yourself; for you who judge practice the same things.... And do you think this, O man, you who judge those practicing such things, and doing the same, that you will escape the judgment of God?" (Romans 2:1, 3).

Each person has the light of creation and the light of conscience.

That's enough to condemn everyone in the world, not for what that person doesn't know and hasn't done, but for what he or she does know and has done.

There is also the light of Christ. Not everyone in the world has that. Christ's light is what is necessary to receive grace and mercy rather than simply justice. It's our responsibility to share the gospel of Christ with others. That is the message of Romans 3.

So there it is. In addition to His Word, God reveals Himself through the light of creation, the light of conscience, and the light of Christ. As a result, no one will be condemned for not believing in a Christ he never knew. He will be condemned for his idolatry in rejecting the God he did know, for his ingratitude for God's gifts, for his violation of the conscience God has placed within that person's heart, and for the sins he has committed that he knew to be wrong.

I have asked people from all over the world, from every kind of religious background, this question: Have you ever done anything you believed was wrong? Every person has responded exactly the same way. You know what they say? "Ha, ha, ha, ha." They laugh…every time! "Of course, everybody has," they all admit. They know they have done things that were wrong. If, therefore, they condemn themselves, why should they be surprised if God condemns them?

A SMOKE SCREEN?

People sometimes claim to reject Christianity because of the problem of evil. They look at the universe as if they have more compassion than God. They feel that, if God were truly good, He wouldn't allow all these terrible things to happen, especially things done in His name. My response is that those people are looking for an excuse to reject the Christian faith because of the moral claim it makes on their lives. One homosexual protester carried a sign proclaiming, "Get your Bible out of my pants!" That cuts right to the chase. His problem with Christianity has nothing to do with questions about evil; it has to do with his sexual choices.

Jesus put the matter in a nutshell. "Light has come into the world, and men loved darkness rather than light, because their deeds were evil" (John 3:19). That's why people reject Him.

Apart from those who use the problem of evil as a smoke screen to reject the Christian faith, the honest believer (and the honest skeptic) could well struggle with the issue of how a good God can allow evil in the world. This is such an important question that I will deal with another aspect of it in the next chapter: "What about the problem of pain?"

....

CHAPTER 11

What about the Problem of Pain?

Now as Jesus passed by, He saw a man who was blind from birth. And His disciples asked Him, saying, "Rabbi, who sinned, this man or his parents, that he was born blind?" Jesus answered, "Neither this man nor his parents sinned, but that the works of God should be revealed in him."

JOHN 9:1–3

Just recently, a friend of mine attended a funeral. The woman in the casket was only forty-five years old and had been devastated by cancer. The last week of her life, she was lost in pain, morphine, and the ravages of a terrible disease. At the funeral, my friend couldn't keep his eyes off the woman's husband. As the pastor spoke and friends wept and songs were sung, the husband was focused on just one thing—trying to comfort his two daughters, who were eighteen and sixteen years old. The father's pain in seeing his children suffer, the pain that made him want to weep, and the woman's pain as she died of cancer, all remind us of the many forms pain can take.

A six-year-old boy wakes up in the middle of the night. He complains of a headache. In the morning, the headache is worse. In another couple of days, the little boy can hardly stand the pain. His parents take him to a doctor, who finds a brain tumor. In a few months, after much suffering, the boy dies. The parents remember how odd it seemed to pick out the casket. It was so small. That is another kind of pain.

A teenage girl is in her bedroom studying. She is a good student because she feels pride in her accomplishments, but she also studies hard because it gives her a way to flee from her parents' constant fighting and her dad's frequently abusive rage.

As she works through one of her algebra problems, her dad enters the room. He obviously is drunk. She shrinks back into herself.

"Hey, Pizza Face," he yells at her, breaking into a terrible laugh. "Got any hot dates tonight? Or are you just going to kiss those books of yours?"

What this girl is experiencing is still another kind of pain.

The world is a source of endless suffering that comes in a variety of forms—physical, emotional, relational, and spiritual. It erupts as rage, settles in grief, hides in sorrow, or burrows in depression. Few things in life are certain, but pain is one of them.

In a sense, pain is an extension of the problem of evil, which we looked at in the previous chapter. Once again, it's only the Christian God, who is considered to be good, who confronts us with the need for theodicy (defending a just God in light of evil).

A Perplexing Triangle

The first theodicy was not written by Homer or Plato but by Job. The whole Book of Job, which is generally believed to be the oldest book in the Bible, is a theodicy. Job's central question is, "How can evil and suffering exist in the presence of an all-loving and all-powerful God?" Job's lament introduces this perplexing triangle:

- God is all-good.
- God is all-powerful.
- Evil and pain exist.

Many skeptics believe the triangle's existence is illogical and makes Christianity inconsistent.

Let me say this up front: I don't believe an easy explanation can be found for the problem of pain. God, for whatever reason, has not chosen to reveal Himself on this subject. It would be nice if somewhere Jesus had offered a theological discussion of the problem of suffering and, more importantly, its solution. He did not. No religion or philosophy, including Christianity, has a full explanation for why suffering exists, but Christianity comes far, far closer than others to offering one. Some have none at all.

Obviously, with such a complex issue, the topic can't be dealt with in a few short pages. To take a more in-depth and profound look at the conundrum, I would recommend C. S. Lewis's excellent book *The Problem of Pain*. Meanwhile, I do hope in this chapter to provide you with some ideas on how to respond to the skeptic who asks "How could a good God allow pain to exist?"

Humans keep trying to come up with an answer to this profoundly difficult question. That is, in fact, precisely what the disciples, taking their cue from the Pharisees, were doing in the story recorded at the beginning of John 9. Jesus saw a man who had been blind since birth, and the disciples asked Him, "Why, Lord? You have taught us that the heavenly Father is good and all-powerful. Why, then, is this man blind?"

THE SIN SOLUTION

The Pharisees, as was often the case, already thought they knew the answer: sin. They were, in the strictest sense, proposing the solution of legalism. For every bit of suffering, they believed, sin must lurk nearby— either the blind man's own sin or that of his parents. Their simple cause-and-effect answer to all of suffering was sin.

That idea has some element of truth to it. The Bible certainly teaches that some of the results of sin are sorrow, pain, and suffering, but that doesn't mean all suffering and sorrow come from some particular sin. When Adam sinned, he brought all manner of woes on himself, his posterity, and the earth. The curse is not only transmitted genetically to our children, but we also find it in nature, which suffers because of sin's curse and because of our first parent's disobedience.

Jesus repudiated the Pharisees' legalistic conclusion and said that sin was not the reason this blind man suffered. Rather the man suffered so that the works of God could be revealed in him. Here is part of the solution. Theologians classify Jesus' explanation as the "instrumental" argument. The basic reasoning goes something like this: Suffering, in God's loving hands, is used to bring about a greater good.

As every parent knows, children are chastened that they might develop good moral character. What would you say if someone were to ask, "How can you parents claim to be Christians, claim to be good and godly people, and then chasten your child? This is unthinkable. You must be horrible tyrants, abusive parents, to do such a thing." Parents, however, know that unless the child is chastened, his sin nature will prevent him from developing a strong moral character, and he will suffer far more because of his evil deeds.

Clearly, a distinction needs to be made between chastening and punishing. Chastening is done by a parent to better prepare a child for the future. It is correction motivated by love and characterized by gentleness, firmness, and consistency. Punishment is inflicted by a judge on a criminal. It's retrospective, looking back at the crimes he or she has committed. A great difference exists between chastening and punishing. So, the reasoning goes, God uses chastening to help correct, develop, and prepare those whom He loves. It's not punishment.

More Pleasure, Please

The idea of chastening is certainly not popular in today's culture. Our society, for the most part, takes it for granted that the highest goal in life is pleasure. This philosophy, both ancient and contemporary, is called *hedonism*. We might know it by another name today—the *Playboy* philosophy—but it's still the same thing. For those whose primary concern is to obtain pleasure, the presence of pain and suffering is a deep affront.

As Christians, we know—or should know—that pleasure is not the only goal in life. We know that challenges, difficulties, hardships, pain, and suffering are inevitable, but these can be used to strengthen an individual's character and make him or her a better person. With the proper attitude, we can experience Christ's joy in the midst of suffering—a calm assurance that, even though we may not like what we're going through, He is sovereign and will work "all things together for good" for those who love Him.

The Bible also teaches that virtue brings pleasurable rewards, and virtue is the very thing suffering often builds in us. For example, it feels good to live a life that is, in the apostle Paul's words, "above reproach." We sleep better at night.

In God's economy, both pain and pleasure have their place. Christ teaches us that if we will be holy, then we will have His joy, which He gives to us. The Bible, however, also calls us to suffer, to voluntarily take up our cross and follow Christ. Ultimately, this balancing act between pain and pleasure ends for the Christian when he or she enters heaven where wonderful blessings await—not the carnal blessings of hedonism, but the rich, matchless blessings of heaven.

When we know that suffering is temporary, we can focus better on the purposes of some of our suffering in the world: to turn us from the wrong path onto the road of righteousness, to strengthen our character, and to reveal Christ's purposes in our lives.

Job's friends, like the Pharisees, offered the legalistic response to suffering. They said that the reason Job was suffering so terribly was because he must be a terrible sinner. If he would just confess his sins, all would be well. You recall that at the end of the book, God severely rebuked these false counselors and blessed Job. In the same way, Christ instructed His disciples about the matter of the blind man. Reasons other than simple sin and punishment existed here.

Another human solution to the problem of the three-sided triangle— God is good, God is all-powerful, and evil and pain exist—is to change one of the sides. The idea of "theistic finitism" is constructed around this idea. This belief was popularized by the Jewish rabbi Harold Kushner in his best-selling book *Why Do Bad Things Happen to Good People?* Kushner, while maintaining that evil existed and that God was still all-loving, concluded that God was finite—not all-powerful. God was doing the best He could. He was even growing and learning, but He hadn't worked things out quite yet. Kushner proposed that we should pray for God, which brings up the interesting question: If we are to pray for God, to whom should we pray? Kushner's conclusion is nothing less than blasphemy, for even the Old Testament informs us that the Jewish God is sovereign and all-powerful.

People still ask the question Kushner posed, "How come bad things happen to good people?" The Bible, however, tells us that none of us is really good, that "all have sinned and fall short of the glory of God" (Romans 3:23). We all have a sin nature. Thus, from a Christian perspective, a more accurate question is "How come good things happen to bad people?" Jesus told us the rain falls on both the just and the unjust (Matthew 5:45).

THE COMPASSIONATE CHRIST

Although we don't know the full answer to the problem of pain, we do know God is concerned about the issue. We see this clearly in Jesus. When He was at Lazarus's grave, Jesus was moved in spirit and troubled. The Greek word describing His emotions is that used to describe a horse snorting, which indicates a great depth of compassion. For a person who is suffering, perhaps what is most helpful is another person's caring—someone who knows his or her pain.

A few years ago, my wife was battling cancer. Thankfully, the Lord saw fit to heal her through modern medicine, but I didn't know at the time how all this would work out. One day as I was visiting my wife in the hospital, deeply concerned, a young minister dropped by. I was in tremendous anguish, and this man, whom I had never seen before, came in and said, "Keep a stiff upper lip."

I about stiffened his upper lip. I thought, *Haven't you learned anything in seminary? Don't you have any idea how to comfort those who are suffering?* Although the Bible asks us to weep with those who weep and laugh with those who laugh, we tend to do just the opposite. We see people weeping, and we tell them to "buck up." This is the opposite of what Christ demonstrated to us, for He was deeply moved by human suffering.

TAKING HIS OWN MEDICINE

We have a God who cares about our suffering, a God of compassion. That is important, but that is not all. The Bible teaches that we also have a God who suffered. He entered into this world and suffered everything we have suffered and more. He even experienced the wrath of hell so we wouldn't have to. Dorothy Sayers, an especially insightful writer, put it well when she said: "For whatever reason God chose to make man as he is—limited and suffering and subject to sorrows and death—He had the honesty and courage to take His own medicine. Whatever game He is playing with His creation, He has kept His own rules and played fair. He can exact nothing from man that He has not exacted from Himself. He has Himself gone through the whole of human experience, from the trivial irritations of family life and the cramping restrictions of hard work and lack of money, to the worst horrors of pain and humiliation, defeat, despair, and death. When He was a man, He played the man. He was born in poverty and He died in disgrace and thought it well worthwhile."[1]

Man needs, said Herbert Hoover, more than a savior. He needs a suffering savior, a captain who can understand him and feel his pain. That is why, sometimes, when Christians lose sight of the human side of Christ's nature (He was both God and man), they begin to emphasize His deity alone. To do so separates the real Jesus from them, and often they will look elsewhere for compassion. We need to keep in sight both Christ's humanity as well as His divinity.

Another purpose of suffering is that it serves as an example of God's character. Jesus said that no one could have greater love than to lay down his life for another. By nature, God is a self-giving God. He loves unconditionally and naturally. Christ's suffering doesn't contradict the idea of love. In fact, it provides the greatest object lesson in history of what true love really is: self-giving. The cross, a device meant for human suffering, has become the very symbol of love. Suffering, put in the correct perspective, can accomplish a greater good by exemplifying the self-giving nature of love.

THIS TOO SHALL PASS

Perhaps the most important thing we should remember about suffering is this: It's temporary. For believers in Christ's work, suffering will not be part of eternity. Christ has revealed to us that some day evil, death, pain, sorrow, and tears will disappear. God will wipe away all tears from our eyes. It's interesting that the Bible doesn't emphasize the origin of evil and pain (though it reveals to us many clues) as much as it emphasizes pain's conclusion—it will be eliminated.

This idea is not found in many religions. Buddha thought the only thing we could do was seek to get out of suffering by entering nirvana. The monistic view of life believes there is only one reality—the spirit, which is God. All other things—the world, the flesh, death, and suffering—are illusion. This is the view of Hinduism, Buddhism, and in the West, Christian Science. It's a pessimistic view that sees life as horrible. The only response we can have to suffering and life is to pretend they don't exist and hope we can get to nirvana. This illusory thinking is rampant in New Age philosophy as well.

Again, the denial of reality is a desperate attempt to change one of the sides of the triangle—this time the side of evil and pain. If you believe that evil and life are a mirage, then you don't have to explain God's being good and all-powerful, and you don't have to deal with the seeming inconsistencies of suffering. You just have to live outside of reality. Most other religions offer no real hope for the conquest of evil and pain.

ALL WE LIKE GOOD SAMARITANS

As Christ's followers, we are to imitate the Good Samaritan (Luke 10). We are to roll up our sleeves and get involved in alleviating others' suffering.

In fact, Christians have been doing this from the beginning down to this very day. Throughout the ages, Christians have been:

- rescuing abandoned babies thrown out by their parents (a common occurrence in ancient Rome and other pagan cultures)
- opposing abortion and providing alternatives, such as the network of some two thousand pro-life pregnancy centers across America today
- founding and maintaining hospitals in all corners of the globe, even in remote and dangerous areas
- providing relief, assistance, and self-supporting projects to alleviate the poverty and suffering across the world
- feeding the hungry and clothing the naked

In fact, I have coauthored a book, *What If Jesus Had Never Been Born?* about these and many other ways Christians throughout history have positively benefited humankind and have greatly reduced suffering.[2] Of course, much remains to be done, but let's not ignore the great progress made thus far.

THE POLITICS OF PAIN

Political evils like the Holocaust also underscore the great need for Christian involvement in the political process. Tragically, we must admit that many professing Christians in pre–Nazi Germany abandoned their role as "salt and light" in that culture and—worse yet—some of them supported Hitler and the National Socialist Party. Most didn't realize, of course, the full extent of the evil to be unleashed, although Hitler warned the world in 1925 through his book, *Mein Kampf,* what he was going to do. A false view of piety—that spiritual matters have no implications in other areas of life, including politics—led many Christians to abandon all politics to the unbelievers. Hitler, Lenin, and Stalin were partly the result of this view.

In contrast to that doleful situation, look at the founding of this country—with all its freedoms and its opportunities to redress and correct societal evils—wherein a Christian view of politics prevailed. A Calvinistic view of man and government was embedded in the Declaration of Independence, the Constitution, the Bill of Rights, the Northwest Ordinance, and all our founding documents. Most of our founding fathers were Christians, though not all, but more importantly, it was a Christian view of human nature that unlocked the freedoms we enjoy here. Knowing what the Bible says about humankind's sinfulness, the founders of the United States built many safeguards into our system so that no one group could lord it over another. They were rightfully distrustful of too much power concentrated in the hands of any one person or group of people. James Madison made this very clear in *The Federalist Number 51:* "But what is government but the greatest of all reflections on human nature? If men were angels, no government would be necessary. If angels were to govern men, neither external or internal controls on government would be necessary. In framing a government which is to be administered by men over men, the great difficulty lies in this: you must first enable the government to control the governed; and in the next place oblige it to control itself."[3]

Thus, the Christian doctrine of humanity's sinful nature led to the Constitution's division of powers, its system of checks and balances, and our resultant freedoms. Other forms of government, without such acknowledgment of humanity's sin nature, have unleashed horrible evils for the "good of the people." This is to be expected. A pagan form of government that allows for dictatorship will lead to oppression, repression, and even genocide. The last one hundred years have provided ample proof of that, as we have seen. Indeed, the great historian Paul Johnson, who also wrote *Modern Times,* writes that the twentieth-century state has "proved itself the great killer of all time"[4] with the communists being the most guilty. The biggest evil we face in the world is at the hands of our fellowman.

Someone may well ask why God doesn't intervene every time one person tries to do evil to another, but the implication of the question is that we are all puppets in God's hands or pawns in a cosmic chess game. In the beginning God gave humankind free will. When humanity chose to sin and rebel against God, it was a real choice made by someone who could have done what was right but instead chose to do what was wrong.

A DEAL WITH THE DEVIL

I can hear someone agreeing that most human suffering is at the hands of sinful people, but what about natural catastrophes? What about hurricanes, tornadoes, floods, earthquakes, and famines (not caused by human selfishness or war)?

All of these terrible events ultimately are a consequence of human sin as well. In the beginning, God's creation was good. Humankind lived in paradise, but Adam and Eve traded it all away in a poor exchange with the devil. They were expelled from paradise. Furthermore, a curse was put on the world because of sin. That curse is manifest in nature, which is now "red in tooth and claw," to quote Alfred Tennyson, but it wasn't that way in the beginning, and it won't be that way later when Christ returns (Romans 8:21–22). Meanwhile, we live on a planet that writhes under God's curse.

Another aspect of natural disasters that should be considered is that perhaps we ought not to live in some places. Humans, in their pride and capacity for poor choices, may be taunting God by dwelling in areas where disasters occur so frequently. To take up residence in such places can be presumptuous, careless, or both. ("You shall not tempt the LORD your God" [Matthew 4:7].)

Hugh Silvester writes in his book *Arguing with God:* "We tend to blame God for natural catastrophes but against this I would argue first, that there is no evidence that God wished us to populate inhospitable areas in the first place. Secondly, that the inhospitable areas have been populated as the result of going away from God and making poor decisions in ignorance. Thirdly, that both ancient and modern man has spoiled and polluted the hospitable areas and is in a poor position to criticize God's provision of environment."[5]

Here again we see how people tend to blame God for the natural consequences of humanity's sin.

THE ULTIMATE HORROR

What is the worst suffering imaginable? I submit to you it's nothing we will experience in this life. The most horrible pain and suffering has to be an eternity in hell, separated forever from God and His love. The Bible teaches that those who reject Christ ("he who does not have the Son of God") will be cast into the lake of fire. Whether this description is symbolic or literal, such a fate can't be anything but a horror. Jesus Himself spoke of the torment the unsaved would endure. It is everlasting, without end.

Skeptics must wake up to the ultimate reality that faces them if they die without Christ. In the context of an eternity of regrets, the issue of suffering will no longer be a theoretical smoke screen they can use to reject the free gift of God's salvation. Instead, suffering will be their lot…without letup…for all time. As long as a person is alive, however, he or she still has time to turn from sin and receive Christ as Savior and Lord, an issue I will address in our final chapter.

In the meantime, how are we to respond when a non-Christian tells us he doesn't believe in God because of the pain and evil in the world? I think we need to remind him:

- All suffering ultimately circles back to humankind's sin (though not necessarily that of the sufferer). No one is sinless except Jesus, and He suffered so we wouldn't have to suffer eternally for our sins.
- Why do bad things happen to good people? There are no truly good people—we are all sinful.

- We can learn and grow through suffering. Pain can yield positive results in character development.
- Jesus Christ, in sharing our humanity, has shared in our suffering. He knows the pain and sorrows of slander, persecution, betrayal, torture, and death firsthand. As one of my staff members once put it, "There's no one in the world who is undergoing some sorrow or rejection who can't look to Christ for help, strength, and encouragement."
- We can and must help alleviate others' suffering. Often a skeptic will bring up the objection of the problem of pain but then won't lift a finger to help feed the hungry or clothe the naked. Meanwhile, across America and all around the world, Christians are engaged actively in comforting the afflicted. From Mother Teresa to World Vision, from the Salvation Army to Compassion International, from the benevolence funds and food giveaways of our local churches to the unsung millions of believers who, without fanfare, reach out to comfort someone on a daily basis, the sun never sets on Christians helping the poor and suffering.

The next time someone brings up the problem of suffering, you would do well to remind him or her of these things. Above all, it's important to grasp that human suffering is ultimately caused by human sin, and God nailed that problem to the cross two thousand years ago.

....

CHAPTER 12

Is There Life after Death?

For since by man came death, by Man also came the resurrection of the dead.
For as in Adam all die, even so in Christ all shall be made alive.
1 CORINTHIANS 15:21–22

The man who was dying was the father of one of the original elders in our church. A doctor was in the room, listening for the man's heartbeat, waiting on the imminently inevitable. The dying man, who had been in a coma, suddenly opened his eyes. The doctor, an unbeliever, was amazed at how bright the man's eyes were. That was unexpected in a man just waking from a coma.

The dying man began to look intently at the ceiling. Then, without warning, he stuck his hand out and grasped at the air as if he were shaking someone's hand. Then he reached again, in a slightly different direction, and then again. A smile covered his face. He even laughed once. The doctor, quite shaken by now, turned his head and looked at the spot on the ceiling where the dying man's focus was so intently glued. Of course, the doctor saw nothing. As the man drew his final, labored breaths, still smiling, he began to mumble names—the names of Christian friends and loved ones he had lost long ago. He was entering heaven—shaking hands, reuniting, laughing. His tears were all wiped away, and the disease that had wasted him wasn't even a bad memory. He was finally home. Where he truly belonged.

For the Christian, heaven—with its boundless joy, rediscovered relationships, and blissful worship of God—is where it all ends…and begins. Contrast the idea of heaven—the resurrection to a new life that is the foundation of Christian belief—with the thinking of much of this world. In *Why I Am Not a Christian*, humanist Bertrand Russell writes:

> Man is the product of causes which had no prevision of the end they were achieving,…his origin, his growth, his hopes and fears, his loves and his beliefs are but the outcome of accidental connocations of atoms,…no fire, no heroism, no intensity of thought and feeling can preserve an individual life beyond the grave, and…all the labor of the ages, all the devotion, all of the inspiration, all the noonday brightness of human genius are destined to extinction in the vast death of the solar system. The whole temple of man's achievement must inevitably be buried beneath the debris of a universe in ruins. All these things, if not quite beyond dispute, are yet so nearly certain that no philosophy that rejects them can hope to stand. Only within the scaffolding of these truths, only on the firm foundation of unyielding despair can the soul's habitation henceforth be safely built.[1]

TOO BAD TO BE TRUE

Skeptics believe Christians are not realistic. They accuse us of using religion as a crutch for our weaknesses, and they think the idea of heaven is no more than pie in the sky. What they are asking is simple: "Isn't Christianity too good to be true?" Because it's founded on faith, hope, and triumph, it simply can't be real, they reason.

Certainly, the Christian faith contrasts with what other philosophies and religions think about life. A prominent British humanist states that the most drastic objection you could make about his humanistic philosophy, which elevates man to the position of God, is that it's "too bad to be true." Man is an accident of the cosmos, formed by chance and chaos, directionless in life, and in the end, nothing but food for worms. That is the humanist's viewpoint. What a way to live, and what a way to die.

Meanwhile, most of the other currently vogue religions or philosophies don't add much hope. Hinduism and Buddhism, for example, which are breeding many of the "newer" religions often classified as part of the New Age movement, are inherently pessimistic religions. Life is terrible and something from which a person needs to escape. That is always the conclusion paganism comes to because it paints such a ghastly and dreadful picture of life. The best you can do is hope for a way out.

How different this is from the Christian viewpoint expressed in the words of Christ: "I am the way, the truth, and the life" (John 14:6) and "I have come that they may have life, and that they may have it more abundantly" (John 10:10b).

The escape offered by most other religions—nirvana in some form—isn't that much to write home about. Many people confuse nirvana with heaven. The two concepts are worlds apart. In nirvana, personal consciousness ceases. An individual no longer exists but blends into a greater consciousness in the same sense that a drop of paint becomes part of the color on the wall. A separate sense of identity is gone. Not much of a way to spend eternity, wouldn't you agree? Unfortunately, even nirvana doesn't come until the person has escaped from the wheel of reincarnation.

NOT SO GLAMOROUS AFTER ALL

What New Agers don't understand as they adopt the Eastern idea of reincarnation is that coming back to life isn't something to look forward to. To them life, in all its forms, is to be escaped. It's a terrible evil. What makes things even tougher is that, if you mess up in a previous life, you will come back as some lowly creature—a worm, a slug, or a piece of algae. Given all the sins I have committed in my life, I would probably come back as a vulture looking for roadkill. Isn't it ironic that most of these misguided New Agers, who claim to remember a former life, always seem to have been a pharaoh or Alexander the Great or Charlie Chaplin? Wouldn't it be great to turn on one of those cheap talk shows and hear someone like Shirley MacLaine say, "Yeah, I was a cockroach in the sixteenth century. I lived in some pretty snazzy palaces in those days!" Fat chance.

By the way, gentlemen, do you know the punishment for living a cowardly life, according to Hinduism? You come back as a woman. (Ladies, please remember, I didn't say that—*they* did!) Similarly, ladies, if you live an unworthy life, chances are you'll come back as a bird. It's all downhill from there. Something to look forward to, isn't it?

SOUND AND FURY

May I suggest that how a religion or philosophy views the afterlife (or lack of an afterlife) has an incredible effect on how life is lived on planet Earth. Imagine a person who wanted to be a marathon runner. She gets up every morning, puts in ten or twelve miles, stretches, eats carefully, and runs again in the afternoon—all to train for an upcoming race. In her mind, she always has the finish line before her. That is her goal; that is what she is focused on. But what if she were told the race had no finish line? If she wanted to compete, that would be fine, but she would have to run and run and run until she dropped.

The great philosopher Immanuel Kant said that life without an afterlife, like the marathon runner with no finish line, would be an absurd and meaningless joke. It would be, as Shakespeare so eloquently put it, "a tale told by an idiot, full of sound and fury, signifying nothing."

Kant reasoned from the point of ethics. Everyone, he says, realizes right and wrong exist. Without ethics, life becomes meaningless and chaotic. Ethics, however, he rightly reasoned, depend ultimately on justice. Why should we do right rather than wrong if there is no such thing as justice? If justice does exist, then there must be a life beyond death, because it's quite obvious that in this world evil people often prosper and the good often suffer.

Kant didn't stop with an afterlife. This afterlife, where justice is dispensed, must be ruled over by a great Judge. This Judge, unlike human judges, must be absolutely perfect in His knowledge. Therefore, He must be omniscient—knowing all facts, circumstances, and motives—if He is to judge justly. Once He has judged, He must also be omnipotent. He must have the power to enforce His ruling. That, of course, sounds very much like the Christian God, doesn't it? Kant said that without all this, life is meaningless.

Isn't that exactly what our culture has turned into—a meaningless and cruel joke? I have asked many people, "What is your purpose for living?" More times than I care to count I've received only a tragic silence in reply. Others acknowledge utter meaninglessness and seek a life full of disconnected thrills and pleasures. Their philosophy of life is, Seize the moment! Get out of this crazy life what you can. The apostle Paul wrote, "If the dead do not rise, 'Let us eat and drink, for tomorrow we die!'" (1 Corinthians 15:32b). If indeed Christ is still in His grave, the hedonists have it right, but what an empty life it is.

NEVERMORE

Edgar Allan Poe wrote a now-famous poem called "The Raven." To me, it sums up the hopelessness of life without a resurrected Christ. Poe, who is lamenting the death of his beloved Lenore, ends the poem with these tragic stanzas:

> And the Raven, never flitting, still is sitting, still is sitting
> On the pallid bust of Pallas just above my chamber door;
> And his eyes have all the seeming of a demon's that is dreaming,
> And the lamp-light o'er him streaming throws his shadow on the
>   floor;
> And my soul from out that shadow that lies floating on the floor
> Shall be lifted—nevermore!

The place of utter helplessness and hopelessness is the very same place where the modern atheist, the modern evolutionist, the modern agnostic, the modern existentialist, and most of the modern philosophies will lead men—to absolute nothingness.

THE CRUTCH

"That may be," these hopeless people might admit, "but at least we are being honest. We are seeing life for what it really is. We don't need any crutches, any lies, any God-talk just so we can delude ourselves into thinking life has some purpose. Our foundation, as Bertrand Russell wrote, is the 'firm foundation of unyielding despair.' Religion is simply a crutch for weak people, who can't bear to face up to reality."

Is that true? Well, many Christians throughout history could hardly be classified as weaklings. They were all too aware of reality, thank you very much. The early Christians, for example, endured shunning, mocking, slander, illegal search and seizure, false arrest, kangaroo trials with perjured testimony, floggings, beatings, imprisonment, and stonings for their beliefs. They were crucified, burned alive, mutilated by lions, and hung on poles and covered with pitch and used as wicks to light Nero's gardens. They hardly sound like weaklings. Not a single crutch in sight. The history of the Christian church up to this very day is associated with reality—the martyrs' blood has often been the nutrient of growth.

That isn't to say Christians don't know fear. There is one idea that buckles their knees and sets them shaking like the biggest coward. That is the prospect of God's mighty wrath and justice. The Christian God has many wonderful virtues—His mercy, His grace, His kindness, and His love to name a few. But there is the other side of God—His justice, His holiness, His righteousness, His promised judgment to come, His anger and wrath against sin, and His promise to visit wickedness with His own vengeance. These are truly terrifying concepts.

Jesus said to us, "Do not fear those who kill the body but cannot kill the soul. But rather fear Him who is able to destroy both soul and body in hell" (Matthew 10:28).

In fact, it is the atheists and God-deniers who are seeking to escape from reality. In his wonderful book, *The Psychology of Atheism,* R. C. Sproul maintains that atheism is a crutch for the ungodly. Because of their wickedness and ungodliness, they are unable to live in the real universe.

Bertrand Russell, the humanist whom I quoted earlier, is a prime example of this. He lived an absolutely profligate, adulterous life.[2] Being unable to live in the real universe, which contained a just and holy God, he invented an imaginary universe in which there is no God so his conscience wouldn't drive him crazy. You see, the truth of the matter is that atheism is the crutch of the immoral.

HEAVEN WITH HARPS?

The next question from a skeptic is predictable. "But do you really believe in heaven—all that hooey about golden streets, angels, and choirs?" For people growing up in a culture obsessed with the here and now and immediate sensual pleasure, the idea of heaven is indeed foreign. According to one recent poll, only about 70 percent of Americans believe in life after death. Another way of saying that is that nearly 30 percent don't believe in an afterlife. Let me assure you that just fifty years ago that figure would have been more like 2 percent. A sophisticated, modern, and enlightened society, we are told by the experts, no longer believes in the myths about life after death. How do you answer people who believe that heaven is just so much falderal?

There is convincing evidence for an afterlife. First, and we have already touched on this point, is the church's persecution. Christianity, alone among the religions, is based on one solid fact: Its leader rose from the dead. Neither Buddha, Confucius, Mohammed, Mary Baker Eddy, Gandhi, nor any other great religious leader you care to mention can make this claim. What the apostles went forth to proclaim was that Christ rose from the dead. Christ's resurrection was the cornerstone of their preaching. It was for this that they were tortured and so horribly martyred.

Now, psychologists and psychiatrists will all tell you that no one ever died for anything he believed to be a fraud. Although many have died for frauds, they didn't know it. The apostles all claimed to have seen the risen Christ. The largest institution in the world, the only religion that is in every single nation, was founded on Jesus Christ's rising from the dead. Since that time, millions and millions of Christians have died for the same belief. Spilled blood makes a powerful testimony.

CHRIST'S CHARACTER

The second piece of evidence is Christ's character. As we saw in an earlier chapter, even His fiercest enemies testify to His integrity and the impact He has had on the world. He was the only perfect individual who ever lived. His character was incomparable. Yet it was this same Christ who said He would be taken and judged by His own people, that He would be condemned and crucified, and that on the third day He would rise from the dead. It's the same Christ who said, "I go to prepare a place for you. And if I go and prepare a place for you, I will come again and receive you to Myself" (John 14:2b–3a). So the character of the incomparable Christ, the all-holy and only perfect One, substantiates His claim that He rose from the dead and that there is an afterlife.

There is also historical evidence for Christ's resurrection. He was seen alive again not by one person, or two or eight or twelve, but by more than five hundred people at one time (1 Corinthians 15:4–8), most of whom could have escaped martyrdom simply by denying that fact.

There is also experiential evidence. Many people have had near-death experiences and have returned, with very similar details, to tell about either heaven or hell. In fact, I keep a news clipping in my files that testifies of some famous infidels' near-death experiences. Here is a summary of some of those:

- Sir Walter Scott, a name renowned in history, said as he faced his final hours, "I thought there was neither a God nor a hell. Now I know and feel that there are both, and I am doomed to perdition by the just judgment of the Almighty."

- Charles-Maurice de Talleyrand, a famous French statesman, diplomat, and an unbeliever, said, "I am suffering the pangs of the damned."
- Adams, the infidel, said, "I am lost, lost, lost. I am damned forever." His agony was so great that, as he died, he tore the hair from his head.
- Voltaire, the great unbeliever and skeptic, wrote voluminously denying the Christian faith and Christ, but in his last hours, he said, "O Christ, O Lord Jesus. I must die abandoned by God and man." His condition had become so terrible that his associates were afraid to approach his bedside. As he died, his nurse said that for all of the wealth in Europe, she would never watch another infidel die.
- The French author Constantin-Francois de Chasseboeuf, the count of Volney, wrote a book, *Volney's Ruins,* which was a broadside attack on the Bible and Christianity. When Volney was lying on his deathbed, his anguish was something awful to behold. He kept crying out, "My God, my God, my God," until he fell back dead.
- Sir Francis Newport said, "What argument is there now to assist me against matters of fact? Do I assert now that there is no hell while I feel one in my own bosom? That there is a God I now know simply because I continually feel the effect of his wrath? That there is a hell I am equally certain of, having received an earnest of my inheritance already in my own breast."

SEA OF BLUE FIRE

You don't believe in heaven or hell? Neither did they until just before they entered therein. Many other near-death experiences have also been recorded in recent years. Dr. Maurice Rawlings, in his book, *Beyond Death's Door,* tells the story of Thomas Walsh, who was working on building a dam thirty miles from Portland, Oregon. Witnesses said that, while working on a scaffold, Walsh fell thirty feet and landed on his head on another level of scaffolding, then fell fifty-five feet into the water. It took forty-five minutes to an hour to find his body.

Everyone who saw the accident believed he was dead, but it is those moments, Walsh says, that he remembers more clearly than anything in his life. He found himself standing on a beach looking out into a vast and limitless sea of blue fire. He was not in it, but he could see it. It was dark. He could see other people also on the shore, but he knew that soon he would be judged and the blue fire was his destiny. He said aloud, "If I had only known that such a place as this existed, I would have done anything to avoid coming here." He knew there was no hope, no possibility of escape.

In the distance, he saw a figure perfectly composed, clothed in a white robe, whose face was strong and at peace. Even though Walsh didn't know why, he knew it was Christ, and he thought, "If I could just talk to Him, there might be some hope for me." Unfortunately He was moving away from Walsh at an angle, and when Christ was almost out of sight, He turned and looked Walsh in the eye. Christ said not a word. Instantly, Walsh felt the hands crushing on his chest, and he was on his back in a hospital bed. He was alive to tell the story, and he told it for the rest of his life.

There are also near-death stories of the unfathomable beauty of heaven. One believer said that what she remembered most was the joy. She said ecstasy "filled every pore of my body, every organ, every bone, every cell." It was so great, she said, that all the wealth in the world—all the diamonds, sapphires, rubies, and emeralds piled up into a gigantic mountain—would not be enough for her to return voluntarily to this world. The Bible assures us that such a joy as that awaits all of those who trust in Christ.

She returned to join the rest of us on this strange place called Earth, but now she was filled with hope, meaning, and a desire to live life to the fullest right here, right now, for the glory of God. Now she knew that, after the pain of the marathon run, lay the finish line: heaven.

SEEING THE LIGHT

I think a caution is in order regarding these near-death experiences. Sometimes non-Christians have "seen the light." They have been near death and have been drawn to a light.

An acquaintance of mine, a non-Christian woman, is a stroke victim who had had one of these experiences. She saw a light at the end of a tunnel and then was returned to life. Thus she was convinced that when she died (once and for all), she would go to heaven. Unfortunately, this does not align with the teachings of God's Word. I believe that Satan, who we are told can appear as an angel of light, had deceived this woman and others in similar circumstances.

As helpful as these near-death experiences can be to provide evidence that the grave does not end life, such experiences should never dictate theology. They should never be put on the same level as divine revelation. These experiences should always be interpreted through the filter of God's Word.

AN ELEGANT EDITION

Ben Franklin, a man I would assume was not a Christian, had a great wit and much wisdom. He once prepared this epitaph for himself (although, for whatever reason, it was never used):

The body of
B. Franklin, printer
(Like the cover of an old book,
Its contents torn out
And stripped of its lettering and gilding),
Lies here, food for worms.
But the work shall not be lost;
For it will (as he believed) appear once more
In a new and more elegant edition,
Revised and corrected
By the Author.[3]

We must hasten to add that the only real basis for saying something along these lines is if that person had put his or her trust in Jesus Christ alone for salvation. For that person, death is not the end—it's the beginning.

And a very good beginning at that.

....

Good News

"If you abide in My word, you are My disciples indeed. And you shall know the truth, and the truth shall make you free."

JOHN 8:31B–32

Have you ever driven for a long time in the wrong direction? Sometimes this happens on trips when the husband is driving and he refuses to believe his wife, who told him an hour ago that he missed the exit!

C. S. Lewis once made the point that modern man has been heading in the wrong direction (away from God) for a long time. It's time we humble ourselves, admit it, and turn around, heading back in the right direction. I think it's long past due that modern man move away from the skepticism that plagues our age and move back to the Christian faith, which has provided so much of our civilization's framework.

It's marvelous to know our faith is both logical and reasonable—but most importantly, that it's the truth.

In our time together, we have seen how the Bible is reliable and correct and how both natural and supernatural evidence conclusively show the Scripture's authenticity. We have seen how we can know God exists and that He is the source of life. We have seen how Christ is a visible manifestation of the invisible God. We have seen who Jesus is and who He claimed to be, the Son of the living God.

We have looked at some of the questions that plague humankind, such as the problems of suffering and pain. We've also seen evidence that indicates there is life after death, the greatest of which is the promise and fulfillment of resurrection by Jesus Christ Himself.

So what does it all mean?

THE COLLEGE QUESTIONS

Who am I? Why am I here? Where am I going? Have you ever wondered about these and similar questions? Sometimes these are called the "college questions" because that's the age at which angst-ridden young men and women often begin asking them. Unfortunately, most people who ask them never seem to find satisfactory answers. I don't believe those individuals ever will unless they look outside of themselves and direct these same questions to another—to the One who holds in His hands the key to all things—Jesus Christ.

Who is Jesus? Jesus is God the Son. He is the Messiah who fulfilled hundreds of ancient prophecies. He is the Almighty, the Beginning, and the End. In believing and affirming that, you know you are God's creation, born at this time and placed by His will and His design on Earth as His child.

When we know why He came, then we also know why we are here—to glorify Him and to spread His kingdom. Where was He going? Jesus said, "I go to prepare a place for you.... That where I am, there you may be also" (John 14:2–3). We are going with Him to heaven. He's already getting it ready for us and will receive us to Himself as soon as our time here on earth is full. That's where we're going if we know Him as Savior and Lord.

In Christ, we have our answers. We know who we are, why we're here, and where we are going. We can agree with author Stephen Neill, who once said that when Jesus enters a life, then that life is filled with meaning.

THE SOUL'S LONGING

My friend, contrary to what many modern-day skeptics say, God is not dead. Skeptics have never been able to prove that, and they never will.

Those who have come to know Him know that He is very much alive. The reason so many high school and college students commit suicide today is because they believe life has no meaning. They believe life has been robbed of significance, that all there is at life's end is a skull and a pile of ashes. That is just not going to suffice, because the human soul longs for some assurance of a continuing existence that is better and finer. God has placed immortality within our hearts, and we can't get around it. Some have denied it, but what do they have? What are their lives like?

The most militant atheist and skeptic of the first quarter of this century was Robert Ingersoll. A brilliant and eloquent man, he spent his life lecturing against God, Christianity, and the Bible. Then his brother died. What do you do if you are an atheist and a relative dies? Hardly call a clergyman! So Ingersoll said he would preach at the funeral. At the graveside, he made these sad, futile comments: "Whether in midsea or amongst the breakers on the farther shore, a wreck must mark at last the end of each and all. And every life, no matter if its every hour is rich with love and every moment jeweled with joy will, at its close, become a tragedy, as deep, and as dark as can be woven out of the warp and woof of mystery and death.... Life is a narrow vale between the cold and barren peaks of two eternities. We strive in vain to look beyond the heights. We cry aloud, and the only answer is the echo of our wailing cry."[1]

Or consider the most eloquent, original, imaginative, persuasive advocate of atheism who has ever lived—Nietzsche. He fashioned the twentieth century. To him can be attributed the life movements of Hitler, Mussolini, Lenin and Stalin. God is dead, and the blood will flow in the next century, he said prophetically. Interestingly, he spent the last eleven years of his life as a raving madman, totally insane. Life can't be lived without meaning and hope.

In Jesus Christ there is hope. The coming of Christ is good news. The Christian knows that, but to the non-Christian looking in, Christianity may often seem like bad news—a bunch of dos and don'ts. Actually, true Christianity boils down to a relationship between Christ and us. As the true Christian can testify, flowing out of that relationship is a life of love and joy.

THERE'S GOOD NEWS TONIGHT!

When I was a boy, a radio network news announcer named Gabriel Heater began his program every night with the same words: "There's good news tonight!" I have always remembered his words. I don't remember what the good news was, and I don't know of any news anchor today who would have the nerve to begin his program this way. Looking at the news the other day I saw one disaster, catastrophe, and horrible thing after another, in unremitting repetition. There was no good news that night. Actually, there is very little good news, and most of that is ephemeral and passes away quickly.

Thank God, we as Christians celebrate the greatest good news the world has ever heard. It was predicted to our first parents that the seed of the woman [Christ] would bruise the head of the serpent [Satan] (Genesis 3:15). It was promised to the patriarchs, "And in thy seed [Christ] shall all the families of the earth be blessed" (Genesis 28:14b, KJV). It was prophesied by the prophets: "Behold, a virgin shall conceive, and bear a son" (Isaiah 7:14a, KJV). "The desire of all nations shall come" (Haggai 2:7a, KJV).

At long last, He came. God stood up from His golden throne in His palace of crystal and gold, and stepped down into the world, and a baby was born. What a wondrous day that was, and the angel declared it was good news.

To understand and appreciate the significance of this good news, we need to glance back to the garden of Eden when Satan first made a conquest of the human will and brought humanity into cruel bondage to himself. Through that devil-designed deceit, sin entered into the world, and its blight has been on the earth ever since. Sin extinguished the light of God in the soul of humans, cast over humankind a vile garment of shame and guilt, cleaved a great crevasse between God and humanity, and turned like a howling hurricane the garden of Eden into a sin-blasted wasteland. Despair cast its black pavilion over the hopes of humans.

The Sin Question

What has happened to sin? A book by noted psychologist Dr. Karl Meninger bore that title a few years ago: *Whatever Became of Sin?* Turn on any talk show, and if I were a betting man, I would wager you will never hear the word *sin*. It has been declared intolerant and politically incorrect; it's never mentioned. Though we are up to our armpits in sin, the word is unacknowledged. Read the front page of the paper if you want to know if humanity has fallen into sin. There is no doubt about it.

Something that is even more repressed than the reality of sin is sin's consequences. We not only suppose that no sin is left in the world, but also that, most assuredly, there are no consequences of sin. Yet the Word of God boldly states, "For the wages of sin is death" (Romans 6:23a), and all humankind's explanations and all the ignoring of the fact can't do away with that. God has declared it.

Though we don't like to admit it, sin remains deep down in humanity's psyche. A recent book bore this title: *We've Had a Hundred years of Psycho-Therapy and the World's Getting Worse.* Why? The answer is simple: Psychotherapy can't get rid of sin. What can take away our sin? Nothing but the blood of Jesus. We need a Savior.

I think most of us can't really grasp the humiliation involved in the incarnation. Imagine, if you were to condescend, because you so loved worms, to be born in the womb of a worm, and then to live as a worm. Some might say, "Well, that does do spite to my dignity. After all, I am a human being." My friend, the difference between a man and a worm is infinitely less than the difference between the infinite God and the greatest human. Nevertheless, because He loved us so deeply, He became flesh by living as a human in order to reach out to us and break the bonds of sin.

Satan's Number-One Lie

The great lie of the devil is that Christianity is some sort of wet blanket thrown over the flames of fun, but the fun of the world is fleeting and passing at best. The joy that Christ gives is an everlasting joy that wells up within believers like a thirst-quenching spring of water.

Christ brings joy. You will never know real joy until you know Him. Without Christ, all of the world's joy will only turn to ashes in your mouth and lead to despair and death. Why do you think so many unbelievers self-medicate with drugs or alcohol or try to kill themselves? If the devil's lie is true—if apart from Christ there is joy—then why are so many people miserable?

Billy Sunday, an evangelist of a day gone by, said, "If you have no joy in your religion, there's a leak in your Christianity somewhere." Probably, the truth is, if you don't have joy in your religion, you don't have real Christianity at all, because Christ means joy. The Bible tells us that "the fruit of the Spirit is love, joy, peace, patience, kindness, goodness, faithfulness, gentleness and self-control" (Galatians 5:22–23, NIV). Jesus is joy for the human heart.

SATAN'S NUMBER-TWO LIE

Another great lie of Satan is that sin leads to freedom. The very opposite is true. We live in a time in which many people clamor for freedom to do whatever they want, with whomever they want, wherever they want, whenever they want. We see this moral chaos quite acutely in the realm of sexual sin. These modern hedonists have confused the word *liberty* (freedom with self-control) with another word, *licentiousness* (freedom to sin). Although they claim to be free, in reality they are slaves to their passions and slaves to their sins.

Sin is the root cause of a great deal of skepticism. It's not that skeptics have disproved God. It's that God interferes with their sinful choices. Julian Huxley, of the famous Huxley family who championed the cause of evolution, was once interviewed on television. He was asked why evolution was accepted so quickly. Instead of saying something like "the scientific evidence led any rational person willing to look at the facts to come to that conclusion," he said, "The reason we accepted Darwinism even without proof, is because we didn't want God to interfere with our sexual mores."[2]

I almost fell out of my chair when I heard him say that. It reminded me of the old adage: "The Bible will keep you from sin, or sin will keep you from the Bible."

Yet is the freedom to sin true freedom? Recently, on one of our *Coral Ridge Hour* television specials, we interviewed a dozen former homosexuals and lesbians.[3] They all agreed that while there may have been seasons of fun and excitement in their former lifestyle, overall it was a very entrapping way to live. One of them said that if you separate homosexuals and talk with them one to one, they are "wretched," hurting people. Another one told our cameras that when he was an apologist for the "gay" lifestyle, every night he laid his head in shame on his pillow when he went to bed. After becoming a Christian, he was able to express himself without shame or guilt. Thankfully, all of these guests on our program were freed from their sin through the power of the Good News. They admitted that, although they may have claimed to be free in their sinful lifestyle, it was not until they turned to Christ and were freed from their lifestyle that they experienced true freedom.

This same phenomenon is true with other sins as well. Christ frees us from the devil's lies and snares. The one the Son shall set free shall be free indeed!

HAVE YOU EVER BEEN LOST?

Who needs a savior? Well, if you are sick, you need a physician; if you are ignorant, you need a teacher; but if you are spiritually lost, you need a savior.

When I was about twenty-four years old, I was lost for one week. The actual fact is that I had been lost for twenty-four years and just never knew it. For that one week I was spiritually lost and knew that I was lost. It was very uncomfortable. For the first time in my life, I knew that all of my ideas about religion were fallacious. I knew that my idea of attaining heaven by living a good life and following the commandments was hopeless. I knew I was sinful and condemned and without hope at all.

Frequently, ministers ask, "Are you saved?" Instead, I would ask you this question: Have you ever been lost? You see, if you have never been lost, you have never been saved, because Jesus came to seek and save the lost.

Have you come to a place in your life where you know that you are not right with God? Do you know that you are unclean and sinful? Should you come into His presence, as He has said, do you know that He must condemn you because He is just and holy and righteous?

The good news is that He doesn't want to do that. He will condemn you if you ignore the gift of eternal life that He offers us through His Son, but He doesn't want to. The good news is that He offered a Savior who came into this world to take your guilt, your uncleanness, your vileness, and your sins all upon Himself and to endure in His own body and soul God's wrath in your place. That is what a Savior is, and that is exactly what the world desperately needs today. That's what every lost soul needs.

Have you ever been lost? Or have you always supposed yourself to be perfectly all right, thank you...as good as many and better than some...quite religious. There are millions in this country who are religious but lost, and there are even more who are irreligious and lost. Have you ever seen yourself as a lost sinner for whom Christ died?

Muddy Hands and Hearts

Let me tell you something that may shock you if you think you are good enough for heaven. The Bible makes it clear: There are no good men, and there are no good women. "As it is written: 'There is none righteous, no, not one'" (Romans 3:10). If you think you're good, it's only because you are so far out in the darkness you can't see how bad you are.

If I were to stick my hand into mud until it was filthy and black, and then go outside on a moonless night, I could look at my hand and not even know it was dirty. If I came back into the light, I would see its filthiness. If I held my hand under a light, I would say, "Ugh, how foul that is." As we approach the light that is God, we see our uncleanness.

So it was with the great saints of the Bible and of history. The closer they drew to God, the more they recognized their own sinfulness. "I have heard of You by the hearing of the ear, but now my eye sees You. Therefore I abhor myself" (Job 42:5–6b). In Luke 5:8b, Peter says to Jesus, "Depart from me, for I am a sinful man, O Lord."

Augustine's name is rarely mentioned without the prefix *Saint,* but his most famous book is *The Confessions of St. Augustine.* The great saint confessed he was a sinner. So if you have come close to the light, which is God, you see your imperfections and know how unclean you are.

But a stream flows from the mountain of Calvary that can wash away every stain and make you whiter than snow. "Though your sins are like scarlet, they shall be as white as snow" (Isaiah 1:18). That is the wonder of the Savior.

Scripture says it so well: "And you will seek Me and find Me, when you search for Me with all your heart" (Jeremiah 29:13). Are you seeking Him?

Here is the greatest news in all the world: "For God so loved the world that He gave His only begotten Son, that whoever believes in Him should not perish but have everlasting life" (John 3:16). When we know Him and when we continue in His Word, we know the truth, and the truth sets us free.

Is your life empty, meaningless, dull, sad, discouraged? Are you tangled in a dead-end web of humanism and skepticism? Christ is the answer. He is the One who can take away your sin, free you from its power and give you His joy. Won't you heed the good news and receive that joy?

TRANSFERRED, TRANSPLANTED, TRANSFORMED

We come into His kingdom by first turning away from our sins, admitting that we have wronged both God and our fellowman. We must turn from sin and ask for God's forgiveness. He forgives us freely by the power of Jesus Christ's blood and gives us the perfect righteousness of Christ by the power of His resurrection. When we transfer our trust from ourselves to

Christ, God transfers us into His kingdom. We are transplanted from the anemic soil of our own efforts into the rich loam of God's blessing. It's a place where we can bloom and be transformed into all the potential God poured into our seed when He created each of us.

If you have never accepted Jesus Christ as your Savior and Lord, I suggest you stop and pray to God along these lines: *Lord Jesus Christ, I come to You right now. I come seeking You. I want to find You. Come into my heart and make Yourself known to me. Lord Jesus Christ, Son of God, Savior, I repent of my sins, and I receive Your forgiveness for them. Thank You for washing them away. Come into my heart right now. There is room in my heart for You. Fill me with Your everlasting joy. In Your name. Amen.*

If you sincerely said that prayer or something to that effect, then congratulations! This is your spiritual birthday.

No Speculations

Did you know that you can know for sure that when you die, you will go to heaven? Listen to what the Bible says: "These things I have written to you who believe in the name of the Son of God, that you may know that you have eternal life, and that you may continue to believe in the name of the Son of God" (1 John 5:13). That we can know our eternal destination for sure is one of the great truths of the Bible.

That truth has been a comfort to the famous and wise as well as the poor and humble. The brilliant scientist, Michael Faraday, the discoverer of magnetism, was asked on his deathbed, "Sir Michael, what speculations do you have about life after death?"

He replied in astonishment, "Speculations! Why, I have no speculations! I'm resting on certainties! 'I know whom I have believed and am persuaded that He is able to keep that which I have committed unto Him against that day.'" Only in Christianity is there such certainty, and this certainty is based on the veracity of God's Word.

Whether you have walked with Christ for many years or have just begun, let me encourage you to use the material in this book when you share your faith with others. Ask God to bring people into your life with whom you can share these and similar truths.

There might be times in your life when you need to go back to different parts of this book and reestablish some facts or points of logic in your mind. When pain and suffering come into our lives, it's so easy for us to doubt. With the first trouble, we tend to question God's love for us. When the way is just too hard and life gets too tough, we tend to wonder if it's all true, but in the night hours, when all is dark, it's wonderful to know that our faith is built on historical facts and that those who went before us found the faith to hold up to death itself.

Because the Bible is true and because we belong to God, we should examine our lives and our goals and the way we live. Our foremost goal is to glorify and honor God. We do that by:

- living a life worthy of His high calling, by obedience to His commandments, including the command to love God with all our heart, soul, and mind, and to love those people God has placed in our lives
- keeping close to the Lord by daily Bible reading and prayer
- striving for holiness, without which no person can honor the Lord
- bearing witness to others and striving to bring them into the kingdom of God
- making disciples, teaching and encouraging and helping our fellow believers
- keeping our spiritual eyes open to see the good deeds He has prepared for us to do, so that in reliance on the Holy Spirit, we may do them to His glory

Such a life as this will be glorifying to God, and so we will then be able to enjoy Him forever in heaven when our pilgrimage on Earth is over. All of this we know through the Bible, which, as we've seen over and over in our visit together, is verified from many different angles. We can know the truth, and the truth will set us free. That's good news for believers and honest skeptics alike!

Soli Deo Gloria!

Study Guide for

Personal Reflection

and Group Discussion

This study guide may be used for personal reflection or as the basis for group discussion. As you work through each section, you'll want to have a pen, notebook, and Bible at the ready. Prayerfully consider the challenges and questions—they are designed to help you internalize the valuable principles you've learned about (1) the credibility of the Christian experience, (2) defending Christianity in a hostile world, and (3) making the leap from passive understanding to active faith.

CHAPTER ONE
SKEPTICS ARE WELCOME

1. Nearly everyone with a strong, outspoken faith in Christ has at some point waded through the murky waters of doubt and uncertainty. When have you felt distant from God or uncertain of your faith?

2. How did God help you through that situation? What Scriptures ministered to you? How did Christian mentors and friends help or hurt you in your struggle to believe?

3. Think back to the story of *Ben-Hur.* In what ways does the story line reflect Gen. Lew Wallace's skepticism and his ultimate coming to faith in Christ? Why do you think this story, with its strong Christian witness, received such resounding acclaim from society in general and Hollywood in particular?

4. How have you usually responded when someone denigrates Christianity or claims to be an agnostic? What kinds of responses do you think tend to encourage positive dialogue about Christianity? What kinds

of responses tend to alienate doubters and drive them further from the faith?

5.   As heralds of Christ and guardians of the faith, what can we learn from Jesus' response to Thomas as told in John 20:24–29 and from Paul's exhortations in 2 Timothy 2:24–26?

6.   Make a list of skeptical friends and family members. Pray for each one by name, asking God to help you find ways to encourage them to believe the authenticity of the Bible and the claims of Jesus Christ.

CHAPTER TWO
A WORD ABOUT THE WORD

1. In the anecdote that opens chapter 2, a child mistakenly describes faith as "believing something you know is not true." How would you define faith?

2. The author states that "certain matters of faith go beyond reason, but they don't contradict it." Do you agree? Explain your response.

3. Read Romans 10:6–17. What is the origin of faith? What personal challenge do you find in this passage?

4. Do you agree or disagree with the assertion that it's not necessary for a person to believe the Bible in order to be converted? Explain your response.

5.   Which of the pieces of evidence regarding the Bible's authenticity are most impressive to you? Which do you think might stand up well if you were defending God's Word to a skeptic you know?

6.   The next time someone says to you, "I don't believe in the Bible," how will you respond?

7.   Read 1 Thessalonians 2:13. In what ways is the living Word of God at work in your life?

CHAPTER THREE
MIRACLES AND PROPHECIES:
FACT OR FICTION?

1.   Why do you think the miracles recorded in the Bible are so difficult for skeptics to accept?

2.   Taking a position of courageous honesty, is there a miracle that you have questioned? Have you sought answers to your doubts?

3.   Read Mark 9:17–27. How might naysayers try to explain away this miracle? How could you use this passage to encourage a skeptic who's struggling to believe the Bible?

4.   Do you agree with the assertion that some of the Bible is meant to be taken literally and some figuratively? How have you arrived at this conclusion?

5.   How could you use examples of fulfilled prophecy to defend the credibility of Scripture?

6.   Do you know any "Thomas Jeffersons"—people who would accept parts of the Bible, but scoff at all references to the supernatural? How has the information in this chapter prepared you to talk with such people?

CHAPTER   FOUR
BE   READY   ALWAYS

1. On a scale of one to ten, how would you rate your readiness to respond to honest skepticism about the Bible? Can you think of a time when you were caught off-guard and unprepared to defend your faith? Share your experience with the group. Can you think of a time when you feel you defended your faith well? Share that experience too!

2. Why are so many Christians hesitant to defend their faith? How would you respond to the challenge that "Christians are closed-minded"?

3. When do you think it appropriate to defend Scripture, and when is it appropriate to be silent? What part does the Holy Spirit play in the process?

4. Does "being ready" to defend the faith mean that everyone should understand and be able to apply the laws of logic? Why or why not?

Besides using logic, what are some other ways we can defend our faith in Christ?

5. Which of the logical arguments for the authenticity of the Bible seems most convincing to you?

6. What specific steps will you take this week to answer the challenge of 1 Peter 3:15?

CHAPTER FIVE
WHAT DOES GOD LOOK LIKE?

1. Read Psalm 19:1–4a. How does the world God created testify to God's attributes?

2. Imagine that you are talking with an atheist. How would you use the laws of probability to convince him or her that it takes as much faith to believe in evolution as it does to believe in a Creator God?

3. Read Hebrews 2:6–11. How does the significance of the human race change if one believes that our origins are found in primordial slime rather than in the spoken word and will of our omnipotent Creator God?

4. Given the incredible odds against the spontaneous evolution of life, why do you think so many people cling tenaciously to the theory of evolution?

5.   The author states that questions such as "Could God make a rock so big He couldn't move it?" are designed to entrap. What other entrapping questions about God have you encountered? What are some appropriate responses to such questions?

C H A P T E R   S I X
D I D   J E S U S   L I V E ?

1. What do you think motivates people to seek to reduce Jesus to a myth, denying that He ever lived?

2. What effects have skeptics such as Madalyn Murray O'Hair had on our society? What practical steps can we Christians take to counteract their influence?

3. Why do you think the credibility of the Gospel writers is often questioned when the work of other first-century writers is accepted with little argument? How will you now respond if you encounter this argument?

4. Which piece of evidence for Christ's historicity presented in this chapter seems most convincing to you?

5.   After reading this chapter, how would you respond if someone said to you, "I don't believe Jesus ever lived—He's just a myth"?

6.   Quickly look back over the first six chapters. Cite two or three specific ways in which reading *Skeptics Answered* thus far has bolstered your personal Christian faith. Now cite two or three specific points of evidence or logic that you feel have strengthened your ability to respond to skeptics.

CHAPTER SEVEN
WAS JESUS GOD?

1. What kinds of experiences have you had reasoning with Jehovah's Witnesses or members of other cults?

2. Why did Jesus sometimes claim to be the Christ and sometimes avoid making a direct statement about His identity?

3. Quickly scan through one or more of the Gospels in a version of the Bible that highlights Jesus' words with red print. Which actions and statements of Jesus most loudly declare His deity?

4. Read Philippians 2:5–11. According to Paul, who is Jesus?

5. How would you now respond to a person who says, "I believe that Jesus was a great teacher, but not the Son of God"?

6. What makes Jesus unique in comparison to all other religious figures in history?

CHAPTER EIGHT
CHRIST'S SURPRISING CHARACTER
WITNESSES

1. Is it fair to measure a man by the testimony of his critics? Why or why not?

2. What consistencies do you find in the remarks of Jesus' critics?

3. Which of the critics' statements is most remarkable to you?

4. How do you think such a list of learned scholars and philosophers could credit Jesus with being the greatest influence for good in all of history and yet continue in their disbelief?

5.   How could Jesus' own words from Luke 10:21 be used to answer His critics?

6.   How could you use the statements of these skeptics to support Jesus' claims to a nonbeliever?

CHAPTER   NINE
IS   JESUS   THE   ONLY   WAY?

1.   Have you ever had an experience like young R. C. Sproul's, when you felt intimidated and unprepared to defend your faith? Has that experience had any long-term effects on your willingness to enter into dialogue with a person who is hostile to Christianity?

2.   How do you respond to the statement that "In an immoral, ungodly, sinful, and wicked generation, the only 'virtue' that remains is tolerance of everybody's sin"?

3.   In light of John 14:6, when is it right for Christians to be tolerant of others' views and practices? When is it wrong?

4.   What is wrong with the statement, "If Christianity is the only true religion, then all the other religions are completely false"?

5. How does the fact that Christianity is based on the person of Jesus Christ rather than on a set of teachings place it apart from all other religions? How is this significant to you personally?

CHAPTER TEN
WHAT ABOUT
THE PROBLEM OF EVIL?

1. According to 2 Corinthians 5:17, what determines whether a person is a true Christian or a nominal Christian?

2. How do you think nominal Christians have hurt the cause of Christ throughout history? How do they hurt the cause of Christ today?

3. Next time you hear someone blaming Christianity for wars and killing, how will you respond?

4. How do you believe God will judge those who have never heard or understood the claims of Christ? What Scriptures can you cite to defend your view?

5.   Do you agree with the author's statement that people "are looking for an excuse to reject the Christian faith because of the moral claim it makes on their lives"? Explain your answer.

6.   Read 2 Corinthians 5:10–20. What motivated Paul to continue his struggle to convince skeptics of the truth of the gospel? How will this passage encourage you when people seem to look for any excuse not to believe God's Word?

CHAPTER ELEVEN
WHAT ABOUT
THE PROBLEM OF PAIN?

1. What experience, personal or observed, has confronted you with the problem of pain? How does Matthew 5:45b address this issue?

2. What purpose do you think suffering has served in your life? In the lives of your family members?

3. Following Jesus' example, how should Christians respond to the pain of others? To their own painful situations?

4. Read Hebrews 4:15. What does it mean to you to have a Savior who suffered the full range of human pain and emotions?

5. Do you accept or reject the position that all suffering and disasters are, ultimately, the result of humankind's sin? How does Jesus' statement in John 9:1–3 illuminate this issue?

6. The author contends that Christians are and must continue to be part of the answer to pain and suffering in the world. Do you agree with his assertion? Why or why not?

7. What practical steps can you take during the next several weeks to carry out a mission of compassion to someone who is suffering?

C H A P T E R   T W E L V E
I S   T H E R E   L I F E   A F T E R   D E A T H ?

1.   If you could speak to Bertrand Russell face to face, how would you respond to his contention that life must be based on "the firm foundation of unyielding despair"?

2.   This chapter contains several stories of dying saints and skeptics. How do those stories edify your Christian faith? Which examples were most significant to you? Do you know of someone who has had a similar experience?

3.   How does the lack of belief in eternal life affect an agnostic's attitude and approach to the here and now? How does the promise of eternal life affect a Christian's attitude and approach to the here and now?

4.   Based on John 14:2–3; Revelation 4:1–11; 5:11–13; 21:1–4, 11–27, what do you think heaven will be like?

5. Based on Revelation 9:20 and 21:8, what do you think hell will be like?

6. From your reading of this book, how would you respond to the accusation that Christianity is a crutch and that its main tenets are too good to be true?

EPILOGUE
GOOD NEWS

1.   When in your life have you asked the "college questions": *Who am I? Why am I here? Where am I going?* How did you find the answers?

2.   Why do you think speaking of sin has become politically incorrect in our society? If you were speaking to a skeptic, how would you explain sin and its consequences?

3.   How can we debunk the world's view that "Christianity is some sort of wet blanket thrown over the flames of fun"?

4.   Do you agree with Billy Sunday's statement, "If you have no joy in your religion, there's a leak in your Christianity somewhere"? How do you think whining, joyless Christians hurt the cause of Christ? How should we then live?

5. Describe how Satan's "freedom" actually evolves into entrapment and despair.

6. The author quotes Julian Huxley as saying, "The reason we accepted Darwinism even without proof is because we didn't want God to interfere with our sexual mores." To what degree do you think this is true— throughout history and today? Can you cite examples?

7. At the end of the epilogue, the author lists six challenges for people who want their lives to glorify God. On a scale of one to ten, how would you rate yourself as living up to each of those challenges? In which specific areas might the Holy Spirit be prompting you to improve? How will you go about doing so?

8. Read 2 Timothy 1:12. Can you honestly echo Paul's statement? How has the information presented in this book bolstered your faith?

NOTES

CHAPTER ONE

1. Lew Wallace, quoted in Frank S. Mead, *The Encyclopedia of Religious Quotations* (Old Tappan, N.J.: Fleming H. Revell Co., 1965), 59.

CHAPTER TWO

1. Norman L. Geisler and William E. Nix, *A General Introduction to the Bible* (Chicago: Moody Press, 1968, 1988), 388–9.

2. Ibid., 389.

3. A. T. Robertson, *Introduction to the Textual Criticism of the New Testament* (Nashville: Broadman Press, 1925), 29.

4. Josh McDowell, *Evidence That Demands a Verdict* (San Bernardino, Calif.: Campus Crusade for Christ, 1972), 49.

5. F. F. Bruce, *Second Thoughts on the Dead Sea Scrolls* (Grand Rapids, Mich.: Wm. B. Eerdmans Publishing Co., 1956), 61–2.

6. Millar Burrows, *The Dead Sea Scrolls* (New York: Viking Press, 1955), 305.

7. Gleason Archer, *Encyclopedia of Bible Difficulties* (Grand Rapids, Mich.: Zondervan, 1982).

8. John W. Haley, *Alleged Discrepancies of the Bible* (Springdale, Penn.: Whitaker House, n.d.).

CHAPTER THREE

1. Thomas Jefferson, *The Life and Morals of Jesus of Nazareth* (New York: Wilfred Funk, 1940).

2. Lee Strobel, *Inside the Mind of Unchurched Harry and Mary* (Grand Rapids, Mich.: Zondervan, 1993), 37.

CHAPTER FOUR

1. Frederic G. Kenyon, *The Bible and Archaeology* (New York: Harper & Row, 1940), 288.

2. Simon Greenleaf, *The Testimony of the Evangelists: Examined by the Rules of Evidence Administered in Courts of Justice* (Grand Rapids, Mich.: Baker Book House, 1874, 1965), 2.

3. Ibid., 2–3.

4. Ibid., 7.

5. Francis Crick, *Life Itself* (New York: Simon and Schuster, 1981), 79.

CHAPTER FIVE

1. Ibid., 87–8.

2. Walter T. Brown, *In the Beginning* (Naperville, Ill.: ICR Midwest Center, 1981), 3.

3. Erwin W. Lutzer, *Exploding the Myths That Could Destroy America* (Chicago: Moody Press, 1986), 36.

4. Luther D. Sunderland, *Darwin's Enigma: Fossils and Other Problems* (San Diego: Master Books, 1984), 58–9.

5. Ibid., 130.

6. Quoted in Roy Abraham Varghese, ed., *The Intellectuals Speak about God* (Chicago: Regnery Gateway, 1984), 33.

CHAPTER SIX

1. See Gary Habermas, *The Historical Jesus* (Joplin, Mo.: College Press, 1996). This is an entire book demonstrating the historicity of Jesus. See also R. T. France, *The Evidence for Jesus* (Downers Grove, Ill.: InterVarsity Press, 1986).

2. Greenleaf, *The Testimony of the Evangelists,* 7.

3. McDowell, *Evidence That Demands a Verdict,* 85–6.

4. Quoted in ibid., 84–5.

5. Will Durant, *Caesar and Christ: A History of Roman Civilization and of Christianity from Their Beginnings to* A.D. *325, The Story of Civilization,*vol. 3 (New York: Simon and Schuster, 1944), 557.

Chapter Seven

1. C. S. Lewis, *Mere Christianity* (New York: Macmillan Publishing Co., 1960), 56.

Chapter Eight

1. William E. H. Lecky, *History of European Morals,* quoted in J. Gilchrist Lawson, *Greatest Thoughts about Jesus Christ* (New York: Richard R. Smith, Inc., 1930), 82.

2. Philip Schaff, *History of the Christian Church,* vol. 1 (Grand Rapids, Mich.: Wm. B. Eerdmans Publishing Co., 1955), 436.

3. Manuel Komroff, *Jesus through the Centuries* (New York: William Sloane Associates), 406.

4. Charles Darwin, quoted in Earle Albert Rowell, *Prophecy Speaks: Dissolving Doubts* (Takoma Park, Washington, D.C.: Review and Herald Publishing Association, 1933), 91.

5. Ibid., 90.

6. Thomas Huxley, *Contemporary Review,* quoted in ibid., 94.

7. Ibid., 95.

8. George Romanes, *Thoughts on Religion,* quoted in ibid., 96.

9. H. G. Wells in an article in *American Magazine,* July 1922.

10. Ibid.

11. Ibid.

12. H. L. Mencken, "Treatise on the Gods," 1930, quoted in Rowell, *Prophecy Speaks,* 101.

CHAPTER TEN

1. Transcript of Coral Ridge Ministries TV interview with Dr. David Barrett, conducted by Jerry Newcombe on location in Richmond, Va., 19 January 1996.

2. Hitler quoted in Armin Robinson, ed., *The Ten Commandments: Ten Short Novels of Hitler's War against the Moral Code,* with a preface by Herman Rauschning (New York: Simon and Schuster, 1943), xi.

3. William Shirer, *The Rise and Fall of the Third Reich* (New York: Simon and Schuster, 1959), 240.

4. Tom Dowley, gen. ed., *A Lion Handbook: The History of Christianity* (Oxford: Lion Publishing, 1977, rev. 1990), 589–90.

CHAPTER ELEVEN

1. Dorothy L. Sayers, *Christian Letters to a Post-Christian World,* quoted in Lissa Roche, ed., *The Christian's Treasury of Stories & Songs, Prayers & Poems & Much More for Young & Old* (Wheaton, Ill.: Crossway Books, 1995), 97.

2. See D. James Kennedy and Jerry Newcombe, *What If Jesus Had Never Been Born?* (Nashville, Tenn.: Thomas Nelson Publishers, 1994).

3. James Madison, *Federalist Paper No. 51, The Federalist Papers* Clinton Rossiter, ed., (New York: Mentor Books, 1961), 322.

4. Paul Johnson, *Intellectuals* (New York: Harper & Row, 1988), 212–8.

5. Hugh Silvester, *Arguing with God* (Downers Grove, Ill.: InterVarsity Press, 1971), 80.

CHAPTER TWELVE

1. Bertrand Russell, *Why I Am Not a Christian and Other Essays on Religion and Related Subjects* (New York: Clarion Books, 1957).

2. Ibid.

3. Franklin's epitaph, quoted in John Eidsmoe, *Christianity and the Constitution: The Faith of Our Founding Fathers* (Grand Rapids, Mich.: Baker Book House, 1987), 212.

EPILOGUE

1. Robert Ingersoll, quoted in Rowell, *Prophecy Speaks,* 112–3.

2. Lutzer, *Exploding the Myths That Could Destroy America,* 41.

3. D. James Kennedy, *Homosexuality: Your Tax Dollar at Work* (Fort Lauderdale, Fla.: Coral Ridge Ministries-TV, April 1977), 27.

INDEX

....